Basic Painting and Weathering

For Model Railroaders

Jeff Wilson

KALMBACH
BOOKS

Printed in the United States of America

03 04 05 06 07 08 09 10 11 12   10 9 8 7 6 5 4 3 2 1

Visit our website at
http://kalmbachbooks.com
Secure online ordering available

Publisher's Cataloging-in-Publication
(Provided by Quality Books, Inc.)

Wilson, Jeff. 1964-
    Basic painting and weathering for model railroaders /
  Jeff Wilson.
      p. cm.
      Includes index.
      ISBN 0-89024-624-6

    1. Railroads—Models. 2. Painting.   I. Title.

TF197.W4982 2003   625.1'9
                          QBI02-200964

Art director: Kristi Ludwig
Book design: Sabine Beaupré

Contents

Introduction

Painting—especially the thought of using an airbrush—probably scares off more modelers than any other facet of the hobby. In addition, with the high quality of today's factory-painted locomotives and freight cars, many modelers figure there's no reason to learn how to paint and decal their own rolling stock.

This needn't be the case. With practice and some patience painting is a skill that most can learn. And even if you only use factory-painted equipment, there are many ways to improve that equipment with detail painting and additional decals.

This book is designed as a primer for those new to painting, but with lots of information and ideas for experienced modelers as well. You'll find step-by-step instructions in using and cleaning an airbrush, decaling, applying dry transfers, using chalks, and using and caring for brushes.

Paint washes, drybrushing, and creating effects with chalks are shown on projects from simple to complex, covering freight cars, locomotives, structures, and details. The projects in this book are designed to guide you in working on your own models, regardless of scale, era modeled, or road name.

Few of the techniques in this book are my own. They come from observing others' work, discussing techniques with other modelers, experimenting, reading magazine articles, and even stumbling across materials. The one thing they have in common is that, as the photos of the models show, they work for me. Try them for yourself. Remember that the best way to become proficient at something is by doing it, so pick up your brush, airbrush, and other supplies, choose a project, and have at it.

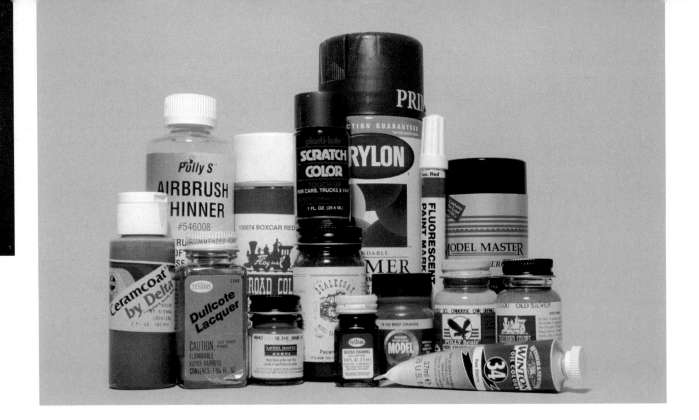

All about paint

Introducing the basics of paint and color

Painting opens up a world of possibilities in modeling. It enables modelers to re-create almost any paint scheme on locomotives, rolling stock, structures, and other items. It also lets us produce various weathering and aging effects.

The world of model paint can be a confusing one, with the wide array of water-based and solvent-based paints available, along with airbrushes, brushes, and other equipment.

We'll take a look at the materials available to us, then take a step-by-step look at using them to make our models as realistic as possible.

PAINT BASICS

In real life paint serves a variety of purposes: It protects surfaces, seals porous surfaces, and keeps metals from rusting, along with the obvious characteristic of providing color. In modeling we generally don't have the same concerns about protective effects, but we're just as interested in getting things the proper colors.

Although color is its most visible characteristic, paint has three primary components: the pigment, which supplies color and opacity; the resin, or binder, which forms the actual paint film; and a solvent, or thinner, which allows the other ingredients to blend and controls the flow characteristics, drying rate, and final thickness of the paint

film. Paint can also contain additives, including fillers, driers, anticorrosion materials, and cleaners.

Paints are designed to dry to a specific sheen: gloss, flat, or various sheens in the middle (usually called semigloss or satin). Choose the sheen you want, and remember that applying a flat paint in heavy coats will not make it glossy.

TYPES OF PAINT

Enamel paints can have either a water or solvent base. Enamels dry by auto-oxidation (by contact with oxygen in the air). Enamels are durable, providing a tough finish. Once dry, they are generally unaffected by their thinners. Enamels should be thinned and cleaned with water (for acrylic enamels) or mineral spirits (for solvent-based enamels).

Lacquers dry by the evaporation of their solvents. They aren't as

resistant to chemicals or thinners as enamels. Use lacquer thinner for cleaning.

Oil paints are still in use; the most common are artist's oil colors, which have many uses in weathering. Clean brushes with mineral spirits or turpentine. Oils can take a long time to dry (a day or two, depending upon how heavy the application).

Acrylic paints are water-based, but once they dry they can't be

dissolved again with water. Don't confuse acrylics with watercolors. Common watercolors aren't the same as acrylics—watercolors will reflow if you apply water to them.

Because of increased concerns over the health risks of many solvents, acrylic paints have become more and more prevalent both in industry and the hobby world. For these reasons most of the projects in this book will use acrylic paints.

MODEL PAINT PROPERTIES

Several companies offer lines of paint specifically for modeling, with colors made to match specific prototype railroad colors. These include Accu-paint, Badger Modelflex, Floquil, Polly Scale, and Scalecoat. These lines also include weathering colors such as mud, grime, earth, rail brown, grimy black, and rust.

Many paints designed for other areas of modeling (such as cars and planes) can be used for model railroading, provided that the color is what you're looking for. These

brands include Humbrol, Pactra, and Testor.

Color is probably the most important property to consider in painting, especially if you're painting a model based on a real locomotive or piece of rolling stock.

Another important factor in modeling is coverage. We want the paint to go on in thin coats, with good color coverage. All of the companies listed above fill this bill, since model paints generally have pigments that are ground finer than many general-purpose paints.

This is the main factor that separates model paints from other commercial paints. Other paints might or might not work, but often the pigment isn't ground as fine, meaning the paint film will be thicker or not as smooth. Be sure to test paints on scrap material before using them on a model.

Good paint adhesion is another important factor. Most train models are plastic, but model paints have to adhere to brass and other metals as well as wood and polyurethane resin.

Fig. 1-1 (above). These two Burlington Northern Santa Fe diesels used to be the same color, but prototype paint fades over time–sometimes quickly, as on the lead locomotive.

Fig. 1-2 (right). Color drift cards issued by railroads and paint companies are used to match colors on prototype equipment.

MATCHING COLORS

Few things start as many arguments—er, make that discussions—regarding painting as color accuracy. Most model paint manufacturers offer paints that have been matched to specific railroad paint colors.

The problem arises when you compare these paints with each other. Inevitably, they will vary a bit from manufacturer to manufacturer. Which one is the perfect match?

A problem is that color perception is largely subjective. What looks like a close match to one person might look way off to another. Keep in mind that viewing colors involves many variables, and matching model colors to photos, slides, or pictures in books is an inexact science.

One main variable is the amount of light. Dark colors, such as many blues and greens, look almost black in dim light. In bright sunlight the color appears brighter.

Thus if you want to paint a model to match the deep blue of the Chesapeake & Ohio, you'll probably be disappointed when you discover that the paint that looked perfect in bright light suddenly looks black when viewed in a dim basement.

Another factor is the type of light. Colors viewed outdoors in bright midday light will look different from those viewed in early morning and late afternoon. Midday light includes more blues, while late afternoon light has more reds and oranges.

The same is true for indoor light-ing. Incandescent lights generally have more reds and yellows, and there are many types of fluorescent lamps available (cool white, soft white, warm white, etc.), each of which gives colors a different look.

Real railroads regulate color by using paint chips and color drift cards issued by paint manufacturers (see fig. 1-2). Even still, paints can fade over time—sometimes quickly and dramatically—as fig. 1-1 shows,

So how do you pick a model color? It's always a good idea to view and compare paint colors in the same type of lighting in which you'll be viewing the model. Pick a color that looks good to your eye when compared to all of the information you have available, and stick with it.

PRIMERS

Some modelers automatically use a primer, regardless of the material being painted or the final color being used. Before you use a primer, it's important to know what primers are intended to do. When using a primer, be sure you pick one that's appropriate for its intended use.

All primers are not created alike. Some have fillers, are sandable, and are designed to fill small cracks or imperfections (Floquil 110009 Primer is one example). Others have rust inhibitors to protect ferrous metal, such as Floquil (110601) and Polly Scale (414293) Zinc Chromate Primer.

Others are designed to seal porous materials such as wood. A good example of this is common household interior (or exterior) latex primer.

Some primers are simply light-colored paints (usually flats) that cover well and are designed to provide a good base coat for light-colored final paints. Examples include Modelflex 1612 Primer Gray and Polly Scale 414134 Undercoat Light Gray.

Don't use a primer with fillers when painting brass or plastic. With those materials, all you need is a primer that provides a uniform color base for your finish coat. If you're painting a light color such as white, yellow, or orange, use a light gray undercoat. Figure 1-3 shows an example.

Many modelers automatically use Zinc Chromate Primer when paint-

Fig. 1-3. The light gray primer over the black styrene helps increase the opacity of the yellow top coat.

ing brass, but it's unnecessary. The primer is designed to inhibit rusting (not a factor with brass), and although it will provide a uniform color, it doesn't stick to brass any better than any other paint. A gray primer is probably a better choice.

MIXING PAINT

Even with the hundreds of different colors available from various manufacturers, it's still sometimes necessary to mix paints to match existing models or prototype paint schemes.

Mixing paint is made more difficult because most model colors are already blends of other colors. Thus, mixing two colors may not give you the exact results you're looking for.

There's no magic solution to the problem of matching existing paint—often a goal when adding detail parts or making repairs to factory-painted locomotives and rolling stock. Use the color wheel and color triangle in fig. 1-4 as guides, and keep experimenting until you find a shade that works.

I like to mix paint in a small aluminum palette, as fig. 1-5 shows. They are inexpensive (look for them

in craft and artist's supply shops), easy to clean, and very handy.

Use an eyedropper to add drops of paint into a well of the palette. Keep track of (write down!) the number of drops in each batch. You can try six different mixes at once using the six-cup palette shown in fig. 1-5. Use a toothpick, tongue depressor, or wood mixing stick to thoroughly mix the paint in each well.

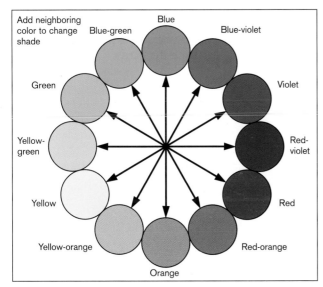

Fig. 1-4. Color wheel

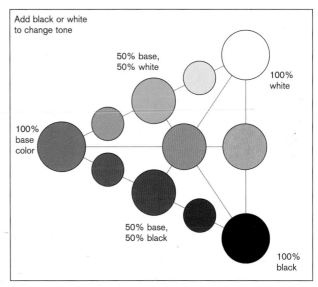

Color triangle

 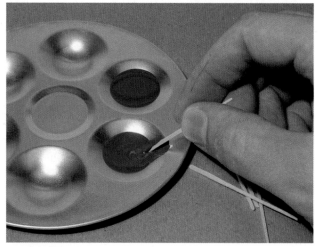

Fig. 1-5. Mix paint in an aluminum palette or other small container. Use a wood toothpick or tongue depressor to stir the paint thoroughly.

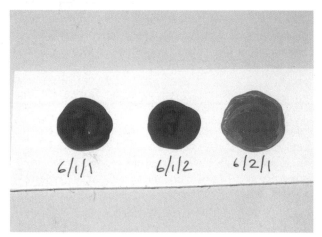

Fig. 1-6. Use a cotton swab to dab a sample of each mix onto a piece of plain styrene.

Fig. 1-7. Use index cards to keep track of paint mixtures that you've used. Include a color swatch, paint formula, and notes on usage.

Once the paint is mixed, use a cotton swab to dab a sample on a piece of plain white styrene, as fig. 1-6 shows, then label these with the mixtures.

It's important to keep track of the paint formulas for anything you paint, such as locomotive or freight car colors. Don't rely on your memory! I keep track of my paint formulas on index cards, as in fig. 1-7. Each card includes a swatch of color, the brand of paint, the formula, and a listing of what the paint was used for. An old recipe card box works well for storing the cards.

MIXING PAINTS AND THINNERS

Each brand of paint usually has its own thinner designed specifically for it. Paint thinners for solvent-based paints are blends of various volatile liquids, such as acetone, methyl ethyl ketone (MEK), toluene, xylene, and various alcohols.

Each brand's thinner is designed to work with that paint's resin to control characteristics such as paint flow and evaporation rate.

Because of this I recommend using a manufacturer's thinner when mixing paint. You might get good results by using common lacquer thinner or mineral spirits, but then again you might not—and there's no sense taking a risk with a model that you've spent many hours on.

By buying these thinners in the economy-size containers (never buy thinner in one- or two-ounce bottles) the price isn't that much more than generic thinner. You can still use common lacquer thinner or mineral spirits for cleanup.

Use water for cleaning up acrylics, and use either distilled water or the manufacturer's thinner when mixing acrylics.

Chapter 2 takes a look at safety when painting. It also looks at airbrushes, brushes, and other equipment that you'll need.

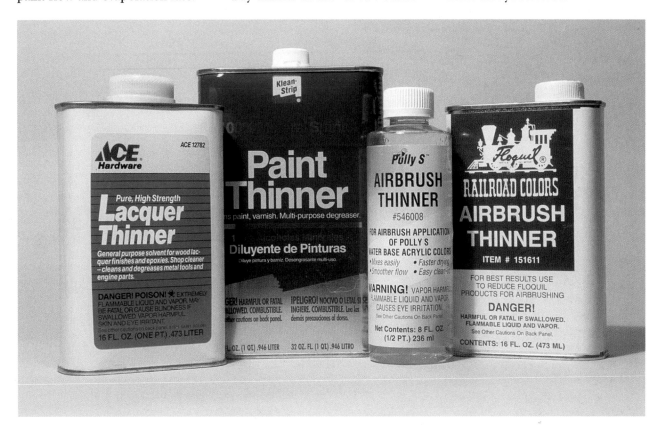

TWO

Tools, equipment, and safety

Working safely with brushes, air supplies, and spray booths

There are many ways to lay down a coat of paint on a model. Airbrushing can be intimidating, especially with the wide variety of airbrushes on the market. Brush-painting, although apparently simple, can become complex with the many types and sizes of brushes on the market.

Sorting through the available products and understanding which ones work best in various situations will make you more comfortable with painting. Let's start by taking a look at the tried-and-true paintbrush.

BRUSHES

Regardless of whether you intend to do finish-painting with a brush or just paint details, you'll find you need several brushes. They come in handy for painting small details, weathering, and painting small and large surfaces, as well as applying decal-setting solution, chalks, and other materials.

Brushes come in many shapes and sizes, and they're made of many different materials. See fig. 2-1. You don't need to buy the most expensive brushes on the rack, but avoid the dime store 10-for-89 cents brushes for anything but applying glue.

The two biggest considerations are brush size and material. Round brushes are measured in numbers:

the smaller the number, the smaller the brush. Number 0 and smaller (00, 000, often called "double-ought" and "triple-ought") are handy for painting small details. Larger brushes are good for painting surfaces, especially irregular surfaces where a flat brush won't work well.

Flat brushes are measured by width. I keep ⅛", ¼", and ½" brushes handy. They're good for painting flat surfaces evenly.

Common brush materials include camel hair, ox hair, sables of various types, and synthetic. Camel and ox hair are generally the least expensive brushes and work well for general-purpose work. For fine finish work, it's tough to beat a

good sable. Chapter 3 goes into more detail on selecting brushes.

Here are some basics for keeping brushes in good shape:

• Clean brushes thoroughly after each use.
• Keep separate brushes for light, dark, and metallic colors.
• Keep separate brushes for applying decal solutions, chalk, and liquid cement.

When a brush begins to show its age, remove it from finish-painting duty and set it aside for use in dry-brushing, other weathering, and scenery work.

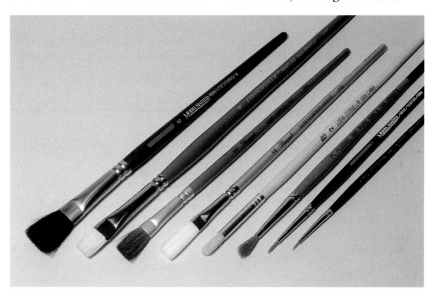

Fig. 2-1. Brushes come in many shapes and sizes. Here's a Model Master ½" black sable, Connoisseur ¼" hog bristle, Floquil ¼" camel hair, ¼" Floquil Silver Fox synthetic, Loew-Cornell no. 2 bristle, Floquil no. 3 pure sable, Model Master no. 0 synthetic, and Kroeger no. 2/0 sable.

CLEANING BRUSHES

A good-quality brush will last for a long time, but the key is to clean it thoroughly every time you use it. Ideally, when you've finished cleaning it, you shouldn't be able to tell which color you just painted.

For acrylics, start by rinsing the brush under warm running water. Put a drop of dish detergent on the bristles and use your fingers to work the detergent gently into the bristles. Rinse the brush again under warm running water, and repeat the process if there's paint remaining on the bristles.

To clean brushes used for lacquer paints, use lacquer thinner; for solvent-based enamels, use mineral spirits. Start by swishing the brush in a jar of thinner. Roll the bristles gently against the inside of the jar to loosen the paint (fig. 2-2). Wipe off the brush on a clean cloth or paper towel, then repeat the process until the brush is clean. Replace the thinner when it gets dirty.

Once you've finished cleaning a brush with either water or thinner, reshape the brush bristles by hand.

See fig. 2-3. If the brush came with a protective plastic cover, use it—unless the cover distorts the bristles. Store brushes bristles-up in a cup or glass, and keep them in an area that's free of dust.

A few cleaning dos and don'ts

• Don't let brushes sit in paint thinner. Prolonged exposure to thinner can dissolve the glue used to hold the bristles in place, and letting the brush rest on the bottom of a container will distort the bristles.

Fig. 2-2. Roll bristles gently against the inside of a bottle of thinner. Don't jab bristles against the bottom or allow brushes to rest in a bottle.

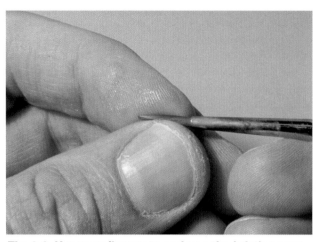

Fig. 2-3. Use your fingers to reshape the bristles once they're clean.

• Don't jab bristles onto the bottom of a container of thinner or water to loosen paint. This damages bristles, causing them to splay.

• Do wet your brush with water or thinner before painting. (Be sure that you wipe off the excess.) This helps keep paint from adhering to bristles, making cleanup easier.

• Do use your fingers to massage the bristles while cleaning with water.

• Do use the appropriate thinner for the type of paint used: water for acrylics, and lacquer thinner or paint thinner (mineral spirits) for lacquers and enamels.

• Don't use lacquer thinner, acetone, or mineral spirits without adequate ventilation.

• Wear protective rubber gloves when using lacquer thinner and other chemicals.

AIRBRUSHES

Airbrushing is the way to go if you want the smoothest, thinnest, and most even finish possible on a model. If you do a lot of painting, you'll find an airbrush to be among your most valuable tools.

Airbrushing scares away a lot of hobbyists (not just newcomers!) but that needn't be the case. As with any physical skill, it takes some practice to become proficient at airbrushing.

Some modelers seem to think that airbrushes are difficult to clean, and that cleaning takes more time than painting. After some practice (and using the proper techniques) you'll find that cleaning an airbrush (especially the external-mix varieties) can be done in just a few minutes. See the sidebar on page 20 for a step-by-step guide.

Chapter 4 looks at airbrushing techniques, but first let's look at the various types of airbrushes available. Quality airbrushes are made by Badger, Iwata, Paasche, W. R. Brown, and others.

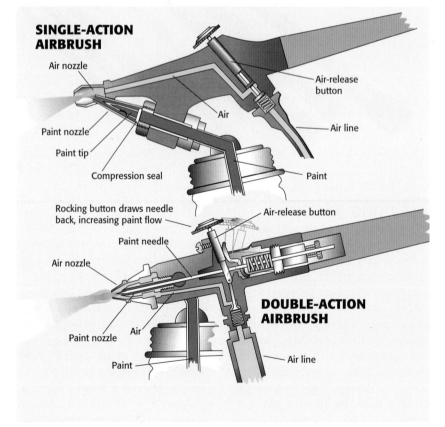

SINGLE-ACTION AIRBRUSH

Air nozzle

Air-release button

Paint nozzle

Air

Paint tip

Air line

Compression seal

Paint

Rocking button draws needle back, increasing paint flow

Air-release button

Paint needle

Air nozzle

DOUBLE-ACTION AIRBRUSH

Air

Paint nozzle

Paint

Air line

Fig. 2-4

External-mix airbrushes

Airbrushes come in two basic styles: external-mix and internal-mix. See fig. 2-4.

With an external-mix brush (fig. 2-5 shows a Paasche H), as the name implies, paint and air are mixed outside the body of the airbrush (see fig. 2-4), at the tip. Air forced across the siphon tube, which extends down into the paint jar or cup (fig. 2-6), draws the paint upward. The paint is atomized at the tip and sprayed onto the model.

External-mix airbrushes are simple to operate and easy to clean, making them ideal for beginners. Since most painting by model railroaders involves using the airbrush like a miniature spray gun (we don't need to paint fine lines or feather paint edges like other plastic modelers), an external-mix airbrush works just fine for most applications.

External-mix brushes have two controls: the air trigger and the paint nozzle. The nozzle screws down onto the paint tip (needle), allowing it to adjust the amount of paint flowing through the nozzle. See fig. 2-7. All external-mix brushes are single-action, meaning that the air trigger controls just one thing: the flow of air.

To use an external-mix brush, start by setting the air at the proper pressure. The paint nozzle should be completely closed. Aim the brush at something away from the model (such as the floor of the booth or a plain card). Press the trigger to start the flow of air, then slowly begin to open the nozzle. The paint will sputter a bit at first, then become an even spray.

It's extremely important to keep the needle tip and nozzle in good shape. If they're dropped or bumped, or if the nozzle is screwed too tightly against the tip, it can be damaged. This can result in poor spray quality or spattering.

Once the spray pattern is smooth, you're ready to begin painting.

Fig. 2-5. This Paasche H is an example of a *single-action, external-mix* airbrush.

Fig. 2-6. A color cup can be handier than a paint jar, especially for small jobs.

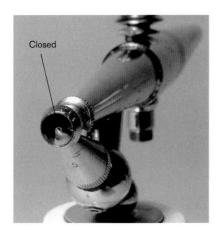

Closed

Open

Fig. 2-7. Unscrew the nozzle on the tip to start the paint flow. The nozzle at left is closed; the one at right is open.

Internal-mix airbrushes

Internal-mix brushes are a bit more complex. The same siphon action draws paint from the jar or cup, but paint and air are mixed inside the airbrush, as illustrated in fig. 2-4. Figure 2-8 shows one model, a Badger no. 155.

These airbrushes can be either single-action—the trigger controls just the air—or double-action— the trigger controls both air and paint flow.

With a double-action airbrush, pushing down on the trigger starts the air flow, and pulling back on the trigger pulls the needle back (fig. 2-9), regulating the paint flow. This allows a great range of control in applying paint.

Although it takes more practice to become proficient with double-action airbrushes because they are more complex, they are extremely versatile, especially when you're doing fine detail work or weather-

ing. Figure 2-10 shows a Badger brush with the needle removed.

The bottom line on internal-mix airbrushes is that they are more complex and harder to clean (and keep clean) than external-mix brushes, but they provide an extremely smooth paint finish with a great deal of control.

I generally use an external-mix brush for most general painting work and a double-action internal-mix brush for most weathering.

Fig. 2-8. This Badger no. 155 is a *double-action, internal-mix* airbrush.

Fig. 2-9. Pulling back on the trigger pulls the needle back within the tip, starting the paint flow.

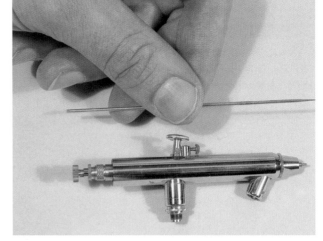

Fig. 2-10. Internal-mix airbrushes have a release screw at the rear. Loosening it allows the needle to be removed from the rear of the airbrush.

SPRAY BOOTHS

Although it's possible to use an airbrush or spray can outdoors, if you do a lot of airbrush painting, you'll find that a good spray booth will greatly increase your enjoyment of painting. A spray booth should be large enough to hold the models you plan to paint. It must be vented to the outside, to remove both paint particulates and any solvent vapor.

When spraying solvent-based paints (either airbrushing or spray cans), it's vital that you do it either outdoors or in a ventilated spray booth. Simply opening the window (even with a fan in it) isn't enough to clear solvent vapors.

A spray booth also clears the area of paint particulates, keeping them from drying in the air and drifting back onto your model (not to mention on you and on other items in your workshop). This is important with acrylics as well as lacquers.

Commercial booths are made by North Coast Models, Paasche (shown in fig. 2-11), and others. The sidebar on page 19 has some information on installing a booth; it also has information on building a booth with specifics on calculating fan capacity and basic construction.

The sidebar on page 19

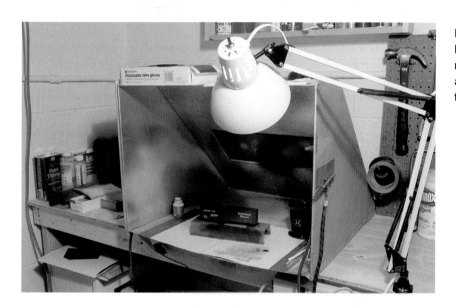

Fig. 2-11. This spray booth from Paasche is large enough to hold most models. The exhaust fan and ductwork are out of sight at the rear.

AIR SUPPLIES

The most economical source of air for an airbrush is a small compressor. Although they can be an expensive initial investment (starting at $100 and up), a compressor will last a long time and give you a consistent, reliable source of air.

Aztec, Badger, Paasche, and others all make small compressors designed for the hobby market. Your most economical choice, however, might be to check out the compressors at a hardware or home-improvement store.

Look for a compressor with a built-in air tank. This lets you paint in relative silence, since the compressor will only run when the pressure in the tank runs low. It also eliminates the "pulsing" that can occur if you connect your airbrush directly to a compressor.

Make sure your compressor has

an air regulator with a moisture trap (see fig. 2-12). Since most air tanks are rated for more than 100 psi, the regulator lets you dial in the pressure needed, usually around 15 to 25 psi.

If you plan to do a lot of painting, you might consider spending the extra money for a silent compressor. As the name implies, they are very quiet, making about as much noise as a refrigerator.

You can also use a stand-alone air tank, filling it with a separate compressor (in a garage) or at a service station. The plus side is that air tanks are relatively inexpensive and painting will be silent; the downside is that you'll have to charge the tank frequently, requiring a lot of hauling the tank back and forth.

High-pressure tanks, such as CO_2 tanks, are another option. They can

be charged to over 1,000 psi and will hold a charge for a long period of time. The downside is that they are much more expensive than a standard air tank, and they still need to be filled periodically—and it will cost you to have them charged. Check with welding, industrial gas, beverage, or scuba supply dealers.

Small cans of propellant, such as Badger Propel (fig. 2-13) are handy and portable, but they are a very expensive air source. Cans will only last for a couple models' worth of painting, and the pressure will vary depending on usage.

Now that you know about the equipment needed, let's learn how to apply a smooth paint finish to a model.

Fig. 2-12. The air regulator allows you to adjust air pressure, and the moisture trap filters out water before it reaches your airbrush.

Fig. 2-13. Cans of propellant are expensive, and it's difficult to regulate the air flow because of varying pressure as the can is used.

Safety

Airbrushing and painting don't have to be dangerous activities, but to keep painting a safe activity, it's extremely important to handle thinners and other chemicals with care.

Until the 1990s, the only viable option for getting a quality paint finish was to use a solvent-based paint such as Accu-paint, Floquil, or Scalecoat. Although there were water-based paints, it was difficult to get consistent results with them, especially when airbrushing.

Today's water-based paints, such as Polly Scale and Modelflex, provide high-quality finishes on models without the worry of solvents. Because of this, most projects in this book use acrylic paints.

Solvent-based paints are still available and can be used safely, but it's important to take precautions to protect yourself. The accompanying chart is a summary of solvents found in several common products.

Product	Solvents contained in product
Accu-paint thinner	acetone, methyl ethyl ketone (MEK)
Floquil Dio-Sol, airbrush thinner	naphtha, toluene, xylene
Scalecoat and Scalecoat II thinner	naphtha, xylene
Testor's Dullcote and other clear coats and lacquers	acetone, toluene, xylene
Common lacquer thinner	MEK, methyl isobutyl ketone, toluene

Exposure to these solvents can initially cause dizziness, nausea, headaches, and fatigue; long-term effects include bone-marrow and blood disorders, nervous-system damage, and respiratory problems.

When you're airbrushing any solvent-based paint, it's vital to do so either in a vented spray booth or outdoors. Simply opening a window—even with a fan in it—is not adequate. Bottom line: If a family member in another room can smell the paint, then you aren't providing enough ventilation.

Even when brush-painting solvents, it's wise to wear a cartridge-style face mask (respirator), as shown in the above photo. A simple dust mask will block paint particulates but won't keep solvent vapors away. Product labels will tell you the type of cartridges needed; generally a TC-23C cartridge, approved by NIOSH or MSHA, will do the job.

A pair of safety glasses is also wise—thinner or paint that splashes in the eyes can cause damage.

Safety with acrylics

Although acrylics are much safer to use than solvent-based paints, they still need to be used with care. Brush-painting is generally safe, but airbrushing releases particulates into the air that can cause respiratory problems if inhaled. It's wise to use a vented spray booth and wear a dust mask or respirator.

If you're thinning acrylics with anything other than water, heed any precautions on the label of the thinner.

Spray booths

When you're designing a spray booth, it's important to make it large enough that any models you'll be working on will fit comfortably in the booth. However, it's also important to keep the booth as small as reasonable, because the larger the booth opening, the larger (and more expensive) the fan you'll need.

The air flow in a booth should be between 100 and 200 cubic feet per minute (cfm), and most fans are rated in cubic feet per minute. To calculate the fan capacity you need, measure the booth opening. Multiply the height and width (in inches) to get the booth opening in square inches.

Next, divide the booth opening in square inches by 144 to get the opening in square feet. When buying a fan, take the fan rating in cfm ÷ the booth opening in square feet to calculate the air flow.

For a fan, use a squirrel-cage type fan with the motor outside of the air flow (old range hood fans aren't suitable). Two examples are the Dayton 4C445A, rated at 525 cfm, and the 2C946, rated at 815 cfm. Other manufacturers offer similar fans.

Always use smooth metal ductwork for venting your booth. Corrugated duct will cut down the fan capacity, and solvents can harm vinyl and other non-metal duct material.

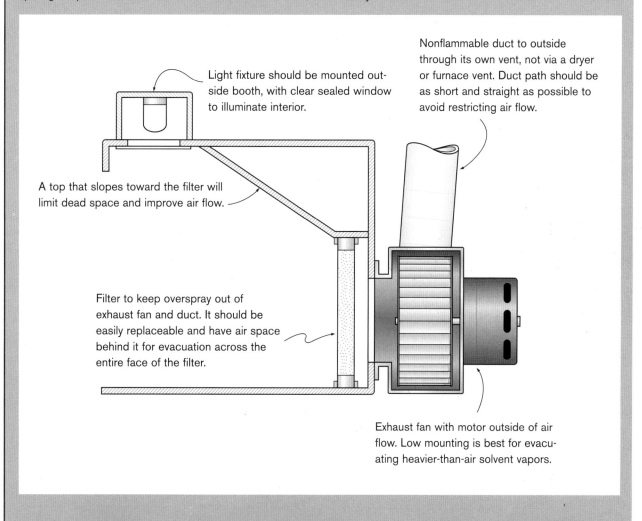

Light fixture should be mounted outside booth, with clear sealed window to illuminate interior.

Nonflammable duct to outside through its own vent, not via a dryer or furnace vent. Duct path should be as short and straight as possible to avoid restricting air flow.

A top that slopes toward the filter will limit dead space and improve air flow.

Filter to keep overspray out of exhaust fan and duct. It should be easily replaceable and have air space behind it for evacuation across the entire face of the filter.

Exhaust fan with motor outside of air flow. Low mounting is best for evacuating heavier-than-air solvent vapors.

Cleaning your airbrush

Airbrushes are precision tools that must be clean to perform well. Old paint in the nozzle, on the needle, in the tip, or inside the brush can cause spattering and poor performance.

To keep your airbrush operating its best, completely clean the airbrush after each use. It seems tedious, but once you get the routine down it only takes three or four minutes—not much, considering the time you've invested in working on a model.

Let's go through the steps, starting with a single-action external-mix brush (a Paasche H in this case) and acrylic paint. If you're using a color cup, dump any remaining paint. I keep an old bottle in my spray booth for this purpose. If you're using a siphon cap on a bottle, unscrew the bottle from the siphon cap and recap the paint bottle.

Place water in the color cup and spray it through the airbrush until the spray comes through clear. (For a siphon cap, place the airbrush on a jar of clear water.)

Remove the color cup or siphon cap from the airbrush and place it into warm water (fig. 1). An old coffee cup left in the booth works well. Use a pipette to force water through the siphon tube several times. Follow this with a pipe cleaner in the water to clean the siphon tube, then use a paper towel to clean the inside of the cup or cap. See fig. 2.

Unscrew the needle (tip)/nozzle assembly. Dip the nozzle into the water, force water through it with the pipette as you did with the color cup, then use a pipe cleaner to further clean it (fig. 3). Be careful not to force the pipe cleaner through the opening, or the nozzle will be damaged. Finish by wiping the nozzle with a paper towel.

Repeat this process with the needle. Again, don't force the pipe cleaner through the top opening in the body of the needle. Use a paper towel dipped in water to wipe the outside of the needle tip thoroughly, as in fig. 4.

Use a cotton swab dipped in water to clean the air nozzle on the airbrush body, as in fig. 5. Blow some air through the brush to clear any water out of the airway.

The initial steps are the same when cleaning an internal-mix airbrush. After removing the color cup or cap, invert the brush and spray it while feeding water through it with an eyedropper, as in fig. 6.

Unscrew the tip and use a cotton swab to clean both ends of it, as fig. 7 shows. Wipe it with a paper towel and set it aside.

Next unscrew the nozzle and use a wet pipe cleaner to clean the passageway from the rear. See fig. 8. Use a piece of wire through the opening to free any paint particles that might be stuck in the opening, as fig. 9 shows.

Use a cotton swab to clean the exposed front of the airbrush,

Fig. 1. Use a pipette or eyedropper to force water several times through the siphon tube of the color cup or siphon lid.

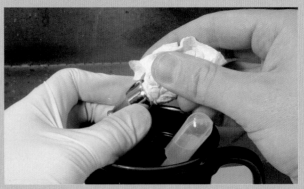

Fig. 2. Use a paper towel to wipe clean the inside of the color cup or siphon lid.

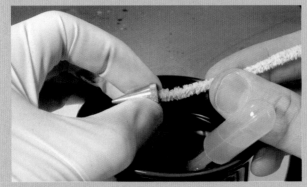

Fig. 3. Run water through the nozzle, then use a pipe cleaner to clean it.

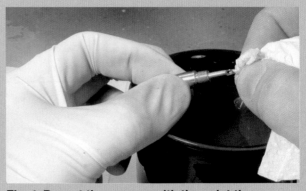

Fig. 4. Repeat the process with the paint tip (needle), then wipe the exterior with a damp paper towel until all traces of color are gone.

then gently clean the end of the needle, as in fig. 10. Be careful not to bump the needle tip—it doesn't take much to damage it. You'll also have to periodically remove the needle from the airbrush (as in fig. 2-10) to clean it.

These steps should be sufficient to clean an airbrush after using acrylic paint, provided you do it immediately after painting. Once acrylics dry, they become even more difficult to clean off airbrush parts than lacquers.

If some color still remains, use super glue accelerator or lac-quer thinner (both with adequate ventilation) to clean any remaining paint. My rule of thumb is that after cleaning an airbrush it should be impossible to tell what color was just painted.

If you're cleaning an airbrush after painting a lacquer-based paint, the steps remain the same, except you'll use lacquer thinner instead of water, and in smaller quantities (in other words, don't leave a coffee cup of lacquer thinner in your spray booth). Use nitrile rubber gloves when cleaning parts in lacquer thinner, and always do it in a vented spray booth.

Fig. 5. Next, clean the airbrush nozzle with a wet cotton swab.

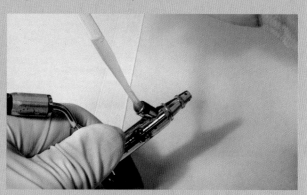

Fig. 6. For an internal-mix brush, invert the airbrush and feed water through it until the spray is clear.

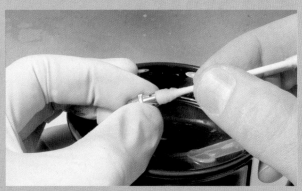

Fig. 7. Clean both ends of the nozzle tip with a wet cotton swab.

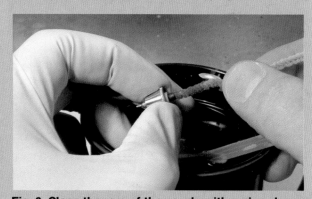

Fig. 8. Clean the rear of the nozzle with a pipe cleaner.

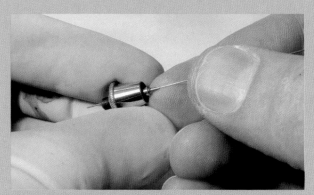

Fig. 9. A piece of wire through the nozzle opening will free any paint particles stuck inside.

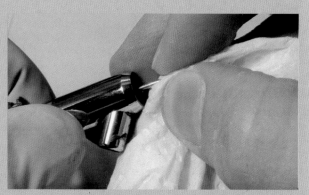

Fig. 10. Clean the end of the needle with water (or thinner as necessary). Be very careful not to bump the fragile tip.

THREE

Putting down a good finish

Getting the best results from brush-painting, airbrushing, and spray cans

The most important step in getting a quality finish on a model is getting a smooth, even coat of paint on the surface. Airbrushing is generally the preferred method of applying paint. Airbrushes provide the finest atomization of paint, providing a thin, smooth coat of paint.

However, if you don't have access to an airbrush, spray cans can still provide a good finish on models. Brush-painting is an essential technique for painting small items and details; it can also provide decent results for finish-painting on models.

Let's start with a look at airbrushing.

AIRBRUSHING

Chapter 2 examined how airbrushes work and explained the different types of airbrushes available. I use both types: a single-action, external mix for most general painting work, and a double-action internal-mix brush for weathering.

If you can only buy one brush, I'd suggest the single-action external mix. They're easier to master, will perform most duties well, and are easy to clean and maintain.

Start by mixing your paint. It's important that paint be thin enough to flow easily through the openings in the airbrush.

The chart in fig. 3-1 shows the recommended mixing ratios and air pressure for various brands of paint. Chapter 1 includes information on mixing paint.

Let's start with using a single-action brush. The photos show a Paasche H, but methods are the same for other single-action airbrushes.

Select the proper nozzle/needle combination. Most airbrushes have three sizes—small, medium, and large—indicated by number or letter. For the Paasche, the sizes are 1 (small), 3, and 5 (large).

When spraying acrylics, use only the large tip. The higher surface tension of water means that it takes more pressure to spray water-based paints than solvent-based paints. Using small nozzles greatly increases the chance that the airbrush will clog. Even when airbrushing lacquers, it's not necessary to use the smaller tips—they are designed primarily for painting fine lines and details.

Another key to preventing clogging is to filter the paint or use a filter on the siphon tube. You can buy commercial stainless steel mesh filters, but I like to use small pieces of pantyhose held in place with a rubber band (the small kind used for orthodontic devices). See fig. 3-2. I keep a supply of these on hand by

the spray booth. When you're done with one, simply throw it away.

Set your air supply to the desired pressure. Be sure the needle is closed all the way. While aiming at a scrap piece, press the trigger to start the air flow. While holding the trigger down, slowly open the needle until the paint begins to flow. When the paint begins to flow smoothly, you're ready to begin painting.

If you're new to airbrushing, practice on a plain piece of cardboard before trying it on a model. Don't press the trigger down while aiming at the model. Instead, begin spraying off to the side, then pass the airbrush with a smooth motion across the surface until you've cleared the other side, then release the trigger. See fig. 3-3.

Proper airbrush distance from the surface will vary depending upon the paint and pressure, but is generally about 3″ to 6″ above the surface. Use your judgment—the

Fig. 3-1 Recommended mixing ratios and application data

Paint	Solvent/water base	Safe to brush on plastic?	Thinner	Airbrush dilution	Airbrush pressure (psi)	Cleanup
Accu-paint	Solvent	No	AP-100 thinner	75% paint, 25% thinner	15-20	Lacquer thinner
Floquil	Solvent	Yes*	Floquil Airbrush Thinner	75% paint, 25% thinner	12-20	Lacquer thinner
Modelflex	Water	Yes	Water	Usually not necessary	25-30	Water
Polly Scale	Water	Yes	Water/Polly S Airbrush Thinner	75% paint, 25% thinner	15-25	Water
Scalecoat	Solvent	No	Scalecoat Thinner	50% paint, 50% thinner	15-20	Lacquer thinner
Scalecoat II	Solvent	Yes	Scalecoat II Thinner	50% paint, 50% thinner	15-20	Lacquer thinner
Testor's Dullcote, Glosscote	Solvent	No	Lacquer thinner	50% paint, 50% thinner	20-25	Lacquer thinner

* Floquil paints made before 1991 (all-red label) or any Floquil paint thinned with Floquil's Dio-Sol thinner may craze plastic. Floquil paints made after 1991 (black-and-red label) and thinned with Floquil Airbrush Thinner are safe to use on plastics.

Fig. 3-2. Use a filter when using a siphon cap on a bottle. Stainless-steel filters (left) work well, but small pieces of pantyhose held with rubber bands are cheap and disposable.

Fig. 3-3. Basic airbrush painting stroke

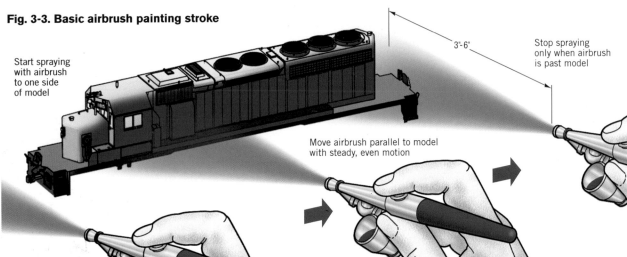

Start spraying with airbrush to one side of model

Move airbrush parallel to model with steady, even motion

3"-6"

Stop spraying only when airbrush is past model

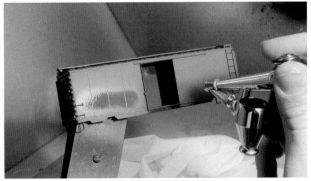

Fig. 3-4. Each airbrush stroke should slightly overlap the previous one. The paint should stay wet on the surface briefly after spraying.

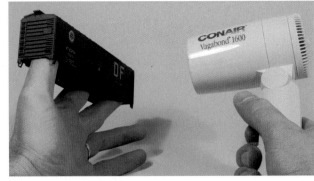

Fig. 3-5. You can use a hair dryer to speed drying time with acrylics, as with the acrylic clear coat on this car.

paint should go on in even coats, as fig. 3-4 shows, with each pass slightly overlapping the previous one. The paint should stay wet when hitting the model, but with no pooling or runs.

In general, acrylics will stay wet longer on a model than solvents, and they may look heavier. This appearance will go away as the paint dries. When using acrylics you can speed the drying time with a small hair dryer, as fig. 3-5 shows.

Go over the model, keeping the hair dryer moving, until the paint dries. Your model is now ready for a second coat of paint.

Apply the second coat in much the same way as the first. Aim the airbrush at different angles to ensure coverage of all details and protrusions on the model. After each coat check the model under a bright light to make sure the surface is completely covered.

Figure 3-6 shows a model with a

good airbrush paint job. The paint is evenly applied on the surface and on details.

Figure 3-7 illustrates what happens when paint is applied too heavily. Paint pools around the details and dries unevenly, causing sag marks and uneven sheen. In extreme cases the paint can run. The only solution for this is to wash the paint off immediately or use a paint remover.

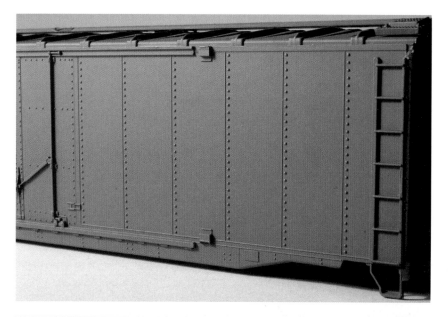

Fig. 3-6. The paint on this boxcar was airbrushed evenly, with complete coverage on the surface and on details. The paint is Polly Scale Boxcar Red, a satin finish.

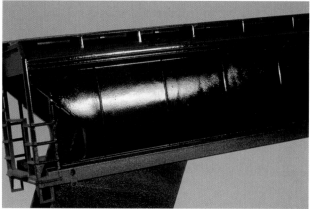 

Fig. 3-7. The paint application on this covered hopper was much too heavy (left). The paint dried with obvious pooling around details (right), an uneven sheen, and a paint run.

Holding models for airbrushing

A painting handle like the one shown in fig. 3-4 and on the cover is a handy tool for holding locomotive and car shells. You can also use cardboard tubes and blocks of wood. Small items can be taped to a piece of cardboard or held with tweezers or pliers. An inexpensive lazy susan placed in a spray booth, as in the accompanying photo, makes it easy to turn items around while painting without handling them.

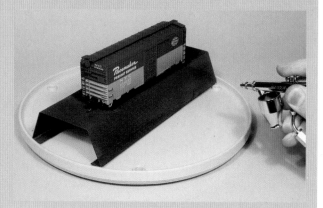

Airbrushing troubleshooting

GOOD FINISH

Problem	Potential causes	Possible solutions
Paint dries before hitting surface; paint rubs off model after drying	• Pressure too high • Spraying distance too far from model • Not enough paint coming through airbrush	• Use lower air pressure • Spray closer to model • Open nozzle wider; use larger nozzle
Paint runs; paint stays wet too long on model	• Spraying distance too close to model • Too much paint coming through airbrush • Paint dilution too thin • Not moving airbrush quickly enough across surface; pausing airbrush over surface	• Move airbrush back from model • Close nozzle opening • Remix paint with less thinner • Keep airbrush moving across surface
Paint peels off model when handled or when you're removing masking tape	• Model surface not cleaned properly before painting • Paint drying too fast when applied	• Strip paint from model; clean surface thoroughly before painting • Make sure paint is wet when it hits the model's surface
Paint doesn't cover well	• Paint dilution too thin	• Remix paint with less thinner
Paint spatters or airbrush clogs	• Dried paint particles in paint • Paint not mixed well or not diluted sufficiently • Dirty airbrush or siphon cap • Pressure too low • Damaged needle or nozzle	• Clean airbrush and filter paint • Mix paint thoroughly; add more thinner • Clean airbrush • Increase air pressure • Replace needle or nozzle
Paint doesn't dry; surface stays tacky	• Paint not mixed sufficiently • Incompatible paint/thinner mix • Reaction between paint and surface	• Strip model with paint remover, remix paint, test on inside surface, repaint model • Strip model with paint remover, repaint with proper paint mix • Strip model if possible (surface may be damaged beyond repair)
Paint crazes or cracks while drying	• Paint applied too heavily and is drying unevenly • Second layer of paint incompatible with first	• Strip model with paint remover, reapply paint in thin coats • Strip model with paint remover; use compatible paint types
Acrylic paint beads up or is repelled from areas on surface	• Surface not clean	• Quickly wash off/remove paint and clean surface thoroughly

SPRAY CANS

Spray cans can also produce good results. The main difference between a spray can and an airbrush is that the paint comes out much faster, and more heavily, from a spray can.

There's a good variety of model paints available in spray cans from Floquil, Scalecoat, Testor, Pactra, and others. Many other non-modeling paints are available, many of which are inexpensive and work just fine for general-purpose use. Just be sure to test them for color and paint film thickness before trying them on a model.

Be sure the paint is mixed thoroughly before painting. Shake the can vigorously for at least two minutes, letting the marble inside mix the paint.

Make sure that the can is warm (at least 70 degrees), or else the paint might not spray properly. You can warm a cold can by setting it in a bowl of warm (not hot) water.

Use the same basic techniques as with an airbrush, but be sure to test

the spray can first to see how fast the paint will come out (every can will be a bit different).

Figure 3-8 shows how. Keep the can about 9″ from the model's surface. Apply the paint in light coats, and let each coat dry thoroughly (at least an hour) before adding the following coat.

As with airbrushing, vary the spray angle slightly to reach all nooks and crannies, and check the model under a bright light to make sure the paint is completely covering the model. Figure 3-9 shows the finished car.

After each coat, clear the nozzle by tipping the can upside down and spraying until no paint comes out. This will keep the nozzle from clogging. You can also use a cotton swab dipped in lacquer thinner to clean the outside of the nozzle as in fig. 3-10.

If a nozzle becomes clogged, you can sometimes fix it by removing the nozzle and using a pin to

remove the clogged paint, as in fig. 3-10. You can also let the nozzle soak in a bottle of lacquer thinner.

Always use spray cans in a well-ventilated area (a vented spray booth or outdoors), and use the same precautions as when airbrushing lacquers.

Brush-painting

Although a brush will never provide as smooth a finish as an airbrush, brush-painting can still give you good results.

Chapter 2 (fig. 2-1) shows a variety of brushes. In general, the softer the bristles, the smoother the finish will be. For painting a finish coat on a model it's tough to beat a good sable. Synthetic brushes will also lay down a smooth coat of paint and will hold their shapes very well.

Camel-hair and ox-hair brushes are less expensive and are a good choice for general-purpose work such as painting rough surfaces and

Fig. 3-8. The can's spray pattern is wider and heavier than an airbrush, so be careful to keep the can moving quickly. Make the first coat a light one.

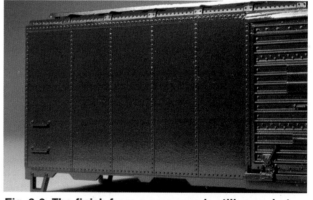

Fig. 3-9. The finish from a spray can is still even, but slightly heavier than from an airbrush. This is Scalecoat Boxcar Red, a gloss color.

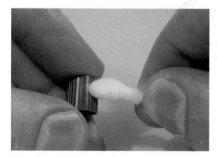

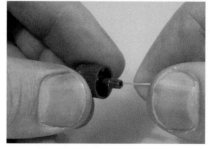

Fig. 3-10. Keep nozzles clean with a cotton swab dipped in lacquer thinner. A pin will often work to remove clogs from the neck of the nozzle.

Fig. 3-11. Use as few brush strokes as necessary to flow the paint onto the surface. Keep the paint edge wet at all times.

Fig. 3-12. Although the finished car shows a few light brushstrokes, brush-painting provides a smooth finish. The paint is Polly Scale Boxcar Red.

Fig. 3-13. Brush-painting is crucial in painting details. Here's an example of using the edge of a brush to paint a raised detail, in this case a molded-on ladder.

weathering. Hog-bristle brushes are stiff and work for specialty uses such as drybrushing.

When brush-painting, use as large a brush as practical for the surface. Start by dipping the brush in water (or thinner for a solvent-based paint) and wiping it off. Wetting the brush prior to painting will help keep the paint from drying on the bristles and will make later cleanup much easier.

Dip the lower third of the bristles in the paint and brush the paint on the surface, as fig. 3-11 shows. Keep brush strokes in the direction of dominant details (rivet lines, ribs, seams, corrugations, etc.). On freight cars, locomotives, and structures it's

a good idea to keep brush strokes in the direction that weathering naturally occurs—top to bottom.

When applying a new brushstroke, apply it to a dry area and brush it back into the area you just painted. This will give you a wet paint edge at all times. This is important, because if you allow an edge to dry, that edge will become visible when it is eventually painted over.

Use as few brush strokes as possible. Let the paint flow onto the surface by itself. Trying to brush the paint one last time will result in visible brush strokes when the paint dries.

Don't try to apply too much paint with the first coat: It generally

takes at least two coats to cover well with a brush. Figure 3-12 shows the finished boxcar with two coats of paint.

It's difficult to get light colors to cover well. Start with an even, light undercoat of light gray before painting a light color such as yellow or orange.

Brush-painting is a vital skill when it comes to painting details, as shown in fig. 3-13 and in the following chapters. I like synthetic brushes for fine detail work—the Model Master no. 0 synthetic is my favorite—because they hold their shapes very well, making it easy to control the paint.

Keeping paint fresh

Air is the biggest enemy of paint—especially acrylics. It's important to keep paint bottles closed whenever possible. If you're brush-painting, pour a small amount of paint into a palette (as shown in Chapter 1) and keep the bottle closed.

There will sometimes be a film of rubbery paint over the bottle opening when you first open it. Remove this, as the photo shows. Also, be sure to keep the cap and threads on the cap and bottle clean, or paint will dry in them (as in the photo of the brown paint bottle) and contaminate the paint with small pieces of dried paint.

One solution shown below (for acrylics) is to use small pieces of plastic wrap. Each time you use the bottle, place a new piece of plastic over the bottle, then screw the cap in place. You still need to wipe the threads clean after each use.

  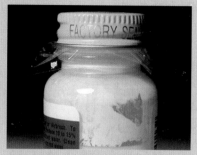

PREPARING SURFACES FOR PAINTING

Modelers deal with many surfaces when painting: Plastic of various types, resin, brass, and wood are the most common. The good news is that today's paints do a good job of adhering to most surfaces. In addition, surface preparation is largely the same regardless of material.

The key for styrene, resin, and brass is that the surface be very clean. Wash the item or model in water with a bit of dish detergent, using an old toothbrush to scrub it. Allow it to dry in a dust-free area.

Don't touch the model with bare fingers after cleaning, or oils will transfer to the surface (see fig. 3-14). Instead handle models from underneath or use latex gloves. Before painting, blow any dust off the surface using an airbrush (with no paint, of course) or canned air.

Some solvent-based paints will etch or damage plastic—notably Scalecoat, Accu-paint (not to be confused with Accu-Flex acrylic, which is no longer made), original-formula Floquil (made before 1991, it has an all-red label), and current-formula Floquil mixed with Dio-Sol.

This generally isn't a problem when airbrushing, because the solvent evaporates quickly before it can damage plastic. However, it's not wise to brush these paints directly on plastic. Use an acrylic or enamel paint instead.

Fig. 3-14. Skin oils from handling can cause paint (especially acrylics) to be repelled from that area of the surface.

Fig. 3-15. Common acrylic primer (in this case from Benjamin Moore) works well for priming wood parts. Keep a small bottle handy on your workbench.

Brass can be treated in much the same way as plastic—make sure the surface is very clean before painting. Some modelers go to the extra step of etching brass models before painting, using either a benchtop sandblaster or a vinegar solution. This gives the paint a bit of "tooth" to hold on to, but I've had good results spraying directly on brass.

When painting brass, make sure the paint goes on wet. It shouldn't run, but it shouldn't appear to dry immediately after contact with the surface. This gives the resin (binder) in the paint a chance to grab the surface.

Urethane resin models and parts often have a very glossy surface, making it difficult sometimes to get paint to adhere. Some paints, especially acrylics, tend to bead up if applied too heavily. Airbrush on resin in very light coats and make sure the surface is extremely clean.

Wood can be painted with any of the commercial model paints, as well as with common household latex paints. Before painting wood be sure to seal it with a coat of sanding sealer or primer (ordinary latex primer works beautifully) as in fig. 3-15. This will keep grain marks from showing through, and

the wood can be lightly sanded after applying sealer or primer.

Wood can warp, especially when painted with acrylic paints. Using primer helps; also, be sure to adequately brace wood structures and models to keep them from warping.

Some structure kits and details (abutments, retaining walls, and the like) are cast in plaster. Plaster is a very porous material that can drink in a lot of paint. Seal the plaster surface with a coat of primer or clear finish before painting it the final color.

Staining wood

Sometimes instead of painting wood we need to make it look like natural wood that has been out in the elements for a while. To do this I like to mix thin washes of acrylic paints, including raw umber (dark brown), burnt sienna (light brown), and mars black.

Squeeze a bit of each color into a pocket of an aluminum palette, then add water. Use a toothpick to mix the paint into the water, but don't mix it thoroughly. This lets you reach down with the brush to grab more or less color as you need it.

Brush the washes onto the wood, starting with the lightest color (burnt sienna) first. Build up the color, following with coats of raw umber and black. Check prototype photos to see how wood ages—the colors range from light grays and tans to nearly black (especially for some creosote-treated wood), with many shades of brown.

The wood trestle shows one completed project. The varied colors of the real wood and multiple stains help give it a realistic appearance.

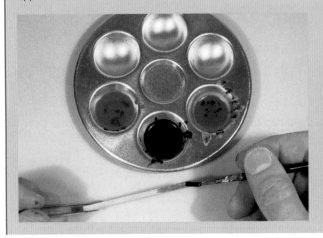

CLEAR COATS

Clear finishes are important in sealing decals and dry transfers, as well as providing a uniform sheen to a car or locomotive. Chapter 4 will show what a difference it makes to add a clear coat to a finished model.

I've had excellent results using Polly Scale's acrylic clear finishes (clear flat, clear satin, and clear gloss). They spray beautifully at 15 to 20 pounds of pressure when diluted 25 percent with Polly S Airbrush Thinner, and they go on clear and colorless. In addition, they have all the other health and cleanup advantages of acrylic paints.

If you prefer lacquers, the old reliable is Testor's Dullcote. Dullcote applied with an airbrush, mixed 1:1 with lacquer thinner, provides an even, extremely flat finish. However, I don't care for Dullcote in spray cans—I find the results too uneven.

For a gloss lacquer finish, use Floquil Crystal Cote mixed 3:1 with Floquil Airbrush Thinner.

If you're limited to spray cans, my favorite is Model Master semi-gloss clear lacquer. It dries very clear and provides an even satin sheen.

MASKING AND MULTIPLE COLORS

When doing a multiple-color paint scheme, the basic idea is to paint the first color, then mask it to spray the second. Apply the lightest color first, followed by the darker color.

To mask the first color, you'll need masking tape that leaves a clean, sharply defined paint edge. The tape must lift off without leaving residue behind and without taking the underlying paint with it. It must also be flexible enough to go around details.

For most modeling work I use common masking tape, as it fits most of these requirements. To ready it for use, stick it to a piece of plain glass, as in fig. 3-16. Cut it with a straightedge and hobby knife to provide a clean, sharp edge.

Apply the tape in small and large pieces as appropriate, as fig. 3-17 shows. Small pieces are easiest to

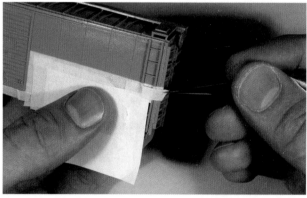

Fig. 3-16. Press masking tape on glass, then cut it with a straightedge and hobby knife.

Fig. 3-17. Apply various-size pieces of tape as appropriate. Paper can be used for large areas.

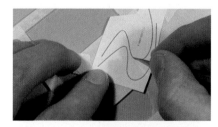

Fig. 3-18. A photocopy of decal striping can be used as an aid in cutting curved masks.

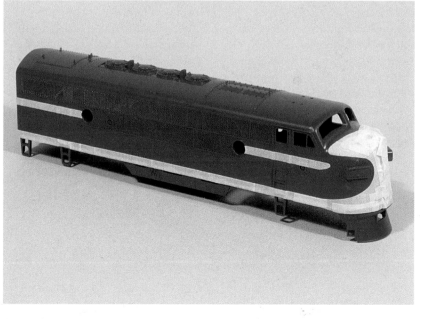

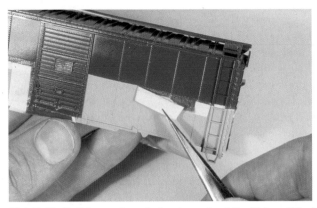
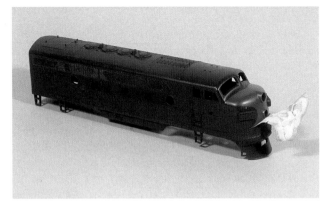

Fig. 3-19. Pull tape sharply back against itself to minimize stress on the underlying paint.

use in tight areas and around protruding details such as doors, ladders, and ribs. Once the paint line is established, you can fill in uncovered areas with more tape, or paper for large areas.

Some schemes require curved lines. The easiest way to cut these is by making paper patterns. Figure 3-18 shows how to use a photocopy of the curved decal striping, cutting through it onto tape to cut the curved masks.

Make sure the tape along the paint edge is firmly against the model before painting. Use the edge of a fingernail or the end of a toothpick or wood stick to burnish the tape in place. Don't

use metal or sharp objects, as they can mar the surface.

When spraying the second coat of paint, keep the airbrush perpendicular to the tape edge. Don't spray toward the tape edge, as it will increase the chance of paint getting under the tape.

Don't allow tape to stay on a model any longer than necessary. Paint the model immediately after masking, and remove the tape as soon as the paint is dry.

Remove the tape by pulling it sharply back across itself, as fig. 3-19 shows. This places the least stress on the underlying paint surface, minimizing the chances of peeling paint.

If a bit of paint creeps under the mask, don't panic. It's usually a simple task to use a brush to paint over it with the proper color. Once the paint dries, the repair won't be visible.

If the tape peels off some of the underlying paint it's generally not the tape's fault—it means that the model's surface wasn't properly cleaned, or that the paint wasn't properly applied (usually that it went on too dry and didn't have a chance to bond to the surface). Touch up the peeled area with a fine-point brush, and it will usually disappear.

OTHER MASKING MATERIALS

Some modelers prefer drafting tape, which looks like masking tape but has less tacky adhesive. I've found that drafting tape peels away too easily (sometimes before you want it to), making it more likely that you'll get "paint creep" than with standard masking tape.

A specialty masking tape that works well is Scotch 3M no. 218 Fine Line Tape (fig. 3-20). It's ¼" wide, has very sharp edges, and is flexible enough to go around details well.

Badger Foto-Frisket is a clear, thin plastic sheet with an adhesive backing. It works well for flat surfaces but is difficult to use on rounded surfaces or surfaces with many protruding details.

Liquid masking products such as Microscale Micro Mask and Walthers Magic Mask are liquid rubber materials designed to be brushed on. Once they harden, they can be peeled away. They're handy for masking in odd corners and areas.

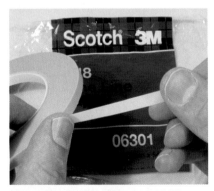

Fig. 3-20. Scotch 3M no. 218 Fine Line Tape is excellent material for masking.

Stripping paint

The best way to approach this is to avoid stripping paint at all costs. The materials and processes are messy, paint removers are expensive, and there are no guarantees that the paint will come off the model as intended.

However, if you absolutely have to strip paint from a model—if you've messed up a paint scheme on a model on which you've put in a lot of time, or if you've found a model that you can't get any other way—you'll have to strip the paint.

The biggest challenge in stripping paint from plastic models is that manufacturers use a wide variety of paints and many types of plastic. What works with one won't necessarily work on another, and a stripper that's safe with one manufacturer's plastic might damage another.

The sooner you strip paint after it's applied, the better your chances at reclaiming the model. If you mess up a paint scheme, getting it immediately into the paint remover gives you excellent odds at stripping the paint cleanly.

I recommend sticking with commercial paint removers. They include Chameleon, Polly S ELO (Easy Lift-Off), and Scalecoat Paint Remover. Other products that work on some paints are denatured alcohol and 91 percent isopropyl alcohol (not the more common 70 percent).

Other materials (such as brake fluid and oven cleaner) may or may not work well, might attack plastic, and can be hazardous to handle.

Whatever type of paint remover you use, wear rubber gloves and goggles (to keep splatters out of your eyes), and work in a well-ventilated area.

Test the paint remover on a hidden area of the model such as the inside of the shell. Brush some on and leave it in place for an hour or more. There should be no signs of crazing.

Stripping paint from brass or other metals is generally easier. You can soak the model in a pan of acetone or lacquer thinner (do this either outside or in a vented spray booth, and cover the container as it's soaking). Make sure there are no plastic parts lurking on the model before doing this.

Fig. 1. Start the process by brushing the paint remover on the surface. Wait until the paint bubbles and peels, then use an old toothbrush to scrub it away. Repeat until the model is free of paint.

Fig. 2. Stubborn paint might require soaking in remover. Proceed in the same fashion, scrubbing away the paint as it blisters and peels. Once the paint is completely stripped, wash it thoroughly in warm water with dish detergent, then rinse and let it dry.

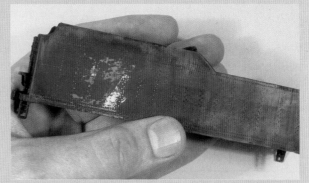

Fig. 3. A few hours of soaking and a good deal of scrubbing removed most of the paint on the side, although the line along the rivets will need more work.

FOUR

Decals and dry transfers

Achieving a painted-on look with lettering and designs

When you're painting your own equipment, decals and dry transfers are the key to achieving a realistic appearance. In addition to providing complete lettering sets, many decals and transfers can help you improve the appearance of factory-painted models. Chapters 7 and 8 show examples of these.

There are more decals on the market than dry transfers, but both have their devotees. Water-slide decals are trimmed from a paper sheet, soaked in water to release the paper backing, and applied to a model. High-quality decals are made by Microscale, Champion, Oddballs, ShellScale, and many others.

Dry transfers—called "rub-ons" in some circles—come on a clear plastic sheet. Rubbing them with a burnishing tool transfers the letters and graphics to the model surface. Manufacturers include Campbell Road, Clover House, C-D-S, Komar, Woodland Scenics, and others.

One advantage of decals is that there's a wide variety of sets available. Also, decal-setting solutions allow decal film to conform to corrugations and rough surfaces. The film can be hidden using clear finish.

The main advantage of dry transfers is that there's no decal film to hide—the lettering is all that transfers to the model. With care they can be applied to rough surfaces.

Let's start by looking at the basics of applying decals.

DECAL MATERIALS

Figure 4-1 shows the basic tools and materials you'll need to apply decals. You'll need a hobby knife with a fresh blade. (Older blades won't cut through the decal film cleanly—the result will be a rough edge that's difficult to hide.) The clear plastic drafting triangle makes it easy to see exactly where you're cutting the decal with the knife. A small, sharp scissors is also handy for cutting out decals.

Also shown are fine-point tweezers to position the decal and soft-bristled paintbrushes for applying water and decal-setting solution. (Be sure to use these brushes exclusively for decals—if you use them for paint, you'll get paint residue on your decals.)

The water dish is a lid from a wide-mouth jar of some type. I like using black (or another dark color), as fig. 4-1 shows—it makes white decals much easier to see if they're floating. The dish can be quite shallow.

While we're on the subject of water: Always use distilled water when decaling. Minerals and other impurities in tap water can leave stains and residues on the model surface (something often mistaken for decal glue residue). Using distilled water results in a much cleaner decal job.

Setting solutions soften decals, allowing them to bond firmly to the model, and helping them fit snugly over details such as rivets, ribs, and batten strips.

Use the setting solutions recommended by the decal manufacturer. Walthers Solvaset and Champion Decal Set are both stronger solutions designed for decals with thicker film. Microscale's Micro Set and Micro Sol are designed for use with thin-film decals.

If in doubt use the weaker solutions—you can always apply a stronger fluid later. Using too-strong solution on a thin decal can cause it to sag or run.

Fig. 4-1. To apply decals, you'll need a knife, scissors, tweezers, brushes, soaking dish, decal fluids, and distilled water.

APPLYING DECALS

For starters, always apply decals over a gloss or semi-gloss surface. Applying decals over flat paint will result in a lot of small air pockets becoming trapped under the decal, as the illustration in fig. 4-2 shows. This will appear as silvering under the decal. Even several applications of setting solution won't solve this problem.

For this example I used an Oddballs Decals Chicago Great Western decal set on an Athearn plug-door boxcar painted Polly Scale Boxcar Red.

The first step is to trim the decal from the paper. Figure 4-3 shows that decals are of two basic types: Microscale decals have film only under the lettering or graphics; most other decals have decal film across the entire sheet.

If the film is only under the lettering, trim outside the film, as the edge of the film will be tapered slightly—a clean edge that will be easy to hide. If the film covers the whole sheet, trim the decal as close to the lettering as possible.

I like to use the small scissors for cutting out around heralds and other odd-shaped decals; the hobby knife and straightedge work well for straight-line cuts. See fig. 4-4.

Use the tweezers to dip the decal in the water for five to ten seconds, then remove the decal and let it sit on a paper towel for about a minute. During this time the decal

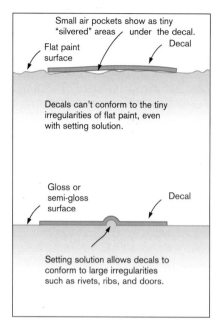

Fig. 4-2. Decals on flat and gloss surfaces.

will release itself from the paper.

With thicker decals, such as Champion and Walthers, you can allow the decal to float in the water until the paper floats off. These decals are sturdy enough to move without their backing paper.

However, I find it easier to keep the decal on the paper when transferring it to the model. It makes the decal easier to position.

Paint a puddle of Micro Set onto the model where the decal will go. Micro Set is a weak setting solution that will soften the decal a bit but will still allow the decal to be moved without damaging it.

Slide the decal from the backing

Fig. 4-3. Microscale decals have decal film only under the graphics; other decals (at right) have decal film over the entire sheet.

paper onto the model, as in fig. 4-5. You can use your fingers, a paintbrush, tweezers, or a toothpick. If using tweezers or other sharp tools, be careful to avoid tearing the decal.

Once the decal is on the model, use a toothpick or brush to prod it into its final position. See fig. 4-6. If it starts to stick, add more Micro Set—don't try to force the decal into moving or you might tear it.

Once you have positioned the decal, the best thing to do is to let it sit until the Micro Set and water evaporate. However, you can use

 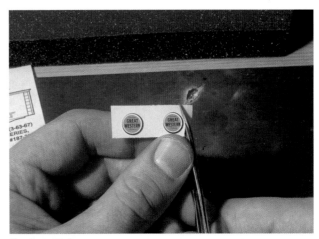

Fig. 4-4. Use either a straightedge and hobby knife or small scissors to cut decals from the sheet.

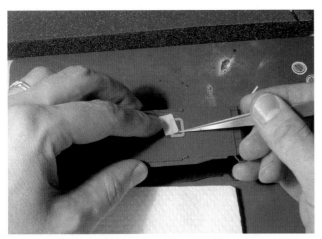

Fig. 4-5. Slide the decal from the backing paper onto a puddle of Micro Set on the model.

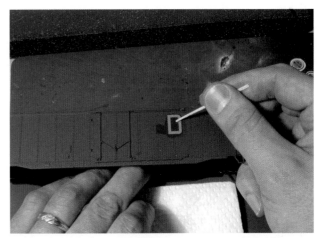

Fig. 4-6. Use a brush or toothpick to position the decal on the model.

Fig. 4-7. You can use the corner of a paper towel to soak up excess setting solution, but at the risk of accidentally moving the decal.

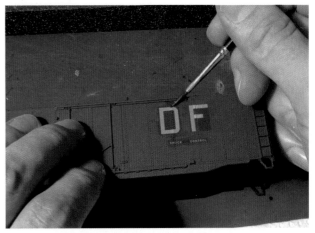

Fig. 4-8. Add Micro-Sol over the decal and around the edges, allowing capillary action to pull the solution under the film.

the corner of a paper towel to blot the liquid away, as in fig. 4-7. There are two risks with this: You could accidentally move the decal, meaning another application of Micro Set; or you could get towel fuzz or other debris on the decal.

Next use a brush to add the stronger decal solution (Micro Sol, Solvaset, or Decal Set). See fig. 4-8. Lightly touch the brush to the edges of the decal and let capillary action pull the fluid under the film.

If you bump the decal out of place, don't panic. Try repositioning it quickly with the brush, and if that doesn't work, use another

brush to flood the area immediately with water. This will stop the action of the solution.

Once the setting solution is applied and the decal is in position, it is vital that you leave the decal alone. Once the strong solution is in place, moving the decal will very likely tear it. The decal may appear to wrinkle, but this is normal. Move on to the next decal, and when they're all in place, set the model aside until it is dry.

Once the decal dries, there will probably be a few air bubbles or shiny areas where the decal didn't properly adhere to the model. See

fig. 4-9. Use a sharp knife to poke these areas, then reapply the decal solution over the surface of the decal. Allow it to dry. Repeat this process until the decal is securely on the model, as in fig. 4-10. When done properly, this process will make the letters and graphics appear painted on, even over surface irregularities such as rivets.

Finish the job by applying a coat of clear finish to the model. This seals the decals and will make the decal film all but invisible. Figure 4-11 shows a model before and after the application of a coat of clear flat finish.

Fig. 4-9. Poke any areas where the decal film didn't adhere properly and add another coat of Micro Sol.

Fig. 4-10. Repeat the setting solution until the decal has completely adhered to the surface.

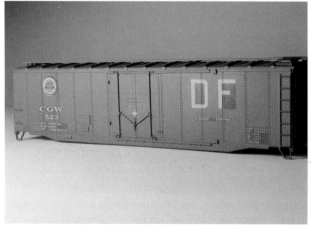

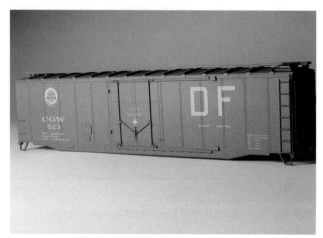

Fig. 4-11. Note how the decal film visible on the model at left disappears (at right) after a coat of clear finish is applied.

STRIPING

Applying decal stripes takes some patience, but with practice and time it's possible to get very good results.

Do stripes in the same manner as other decals, and make sure that the entire surface area is liberally soaked with Decal Set. Long stripes tend to curl when placed in the water. It's okay to let them do this, but try not to let the decal come off the paper. Pull it from the water and press it flat onto a paper towel until it's ready to come off the backing paper.

Slide the stripe from the backing paper onto the model. Once it's on the model, you may have to gently pull it away and reposition it, as fig. 4-12 shows. Here's where some patience is required.

Use a brush to prod the decal into position along its length. See fig. 4-13. I've found the best way to make sure the decal is straight is to sight down the length of the model. You can also hold a straightedge above the surface (avoid bumping the decal) to check alignment

The best situation is where the stripe follows a reference line on the model, such as in fig. 4-13, where the stripe follows the batten strip, or in other situations where stripes follow a paint line.

Once the stripe is in position, LEAVE IT ALONE! Let it dry without touching it. Once it dries, use a brush to gently apply Micro Sol to the stripe. Don't use a brush stroke—instead lightly touch the brush to the edge of the decal at a few locations.

Once again, leave the decal alone until it dries. Repeat the process until it looks as if it's painted on. See fig. 4-14.

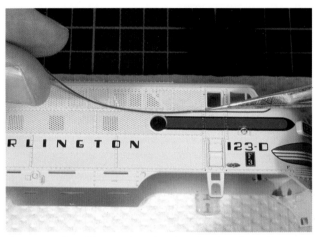

Fig. 4-12. Start by getting the decal stripe into the general area. Use plenty of Micro Set.

Fig. 4-13. Use a brush to prod the stripe into its final position.

Fig. 4-14. The finished striping looks as if it's been painted on.

DRY TRANSFERS

Figure 4-15 shows an HO scale Campbell Road dry transfer set for Chicago & North Western boxcars. The set includes the transfers (the set will do two cars) and lettering diagrams. I applied the set to an Accurail 40-foot boxcar that was prepainted in oxide red and already had the data applied.

Although it's not mandatory, cutting the transfer into manageable pieces makes it much easier to position the various lettering elements.

Cut out the appropriate transfer with small sharp scissors, as fig. 4-16 shows. Treat each block of lettering or graphic as a separate item.

Position a transfer on the model, being careful to get the transfer in proper alignment and position. Unlike decals, you get only one chance to get it right with a dry transfer. Tape the transfer in position, as in fig. 4-17.

Use a burnishing tool to transfer the lettering, as fig. 4-18 shows. The tool shown is from Woodland

Fig. 4-15. This Campbell Road dry transfer set includes the transfers as well as lettering diagrams.

Fig. 4-16. Cutting the lettering into blocks makes the transfers easier to position on the model.

Fig. 4-17. Tape the transfer in place. Double-check to make sure the alignment is correct.

Fig. 4-18. Rub the transfer with a burnishing tool to transfer the lettering to the model.

Fig. 4-19. The lettering will change appearance when it transfers. The "Route of" lettering has been burnished; the logo has not.

Fig. 4-20. Carefully lift the backing sheet. If any lettering starts to pull away, replace the sheet and re-burnish the transfer.

40

Scenics. Hold the transfer to make sure it doesn't slide while you're burnishing.

Use moderate pressure, going over the entire area of lettering or graphics. Move the tool in the same direction as any surface patterns—in this case the vertical rivet and seam lines. Once the lettering has transferred to the model, continue burnishing in all directions.

The lettering will change appearance when it adheres to the model. See fig. 4-19. Go over areas such as rivets thoroughly to make sure the entire transfer has adhered securely to the model surface, and to make sure that the graphics conform to any surface irregularities.

When all of the lettering on the sheet has been transferred, carefully lift the backing sheet, as in fig. 4-20. Figure 4-21 shows how the dry transfers conformed well over rivets and seam lines.

Figure 4-22 shows the completed car. There's no decal film to hide, but it's still a good idea to seal the transfers with a coat of clear finish before weathering.

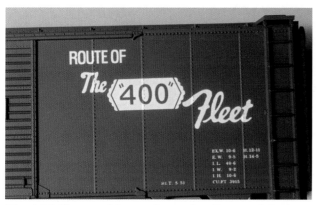

Fig. 4-21. The graphics conformed well around rivets and seam lines.

Fig. 4-22. The completed car shows that dry transfers have no transfer film to hide. It's a good idea to seal the transfers with a coat of clear finish.

Special decals and transfers

Many decal and dry-transfer sets are available besides road name sets for freight cars and locomotives. Possibly the most common "special" sets are alphabet and number sets. They are available in many sizes, colors, and styles, in both dry transfers and decals, from Microscale, Woodland Scenics, Champion, C-D-S, and others. They are great for making signs and customizing road names.

Stripes are also available in many colors and sizes.

Microscale has dozens of sign sets available, and they're also made by Woodland Scenics and others. Some are designed for specific structures (Microscale makes sets designed for the City Classics diner and gas station), but most can be used as-is or modified for virtually any structure, as well as on billboards and free-standing signs.

Clear decal sheets are available from Microscale, Walthers, and others. This is handy for making your own decals, which you can do on a laser printer, Alps printer, or with dry transfers, paint, or gel pens.

A very handy (and often overlooked) set of decals is the trim film sheets made by Microscale. These are sheets of solid colors (several colors are available). They are great for adding color to surface areas without painting. Examples include sign backgrounds, number board backgrounds, locomotive kick plates, and paint patches. You can cut them to complex shapes before applying them like a standard decal.

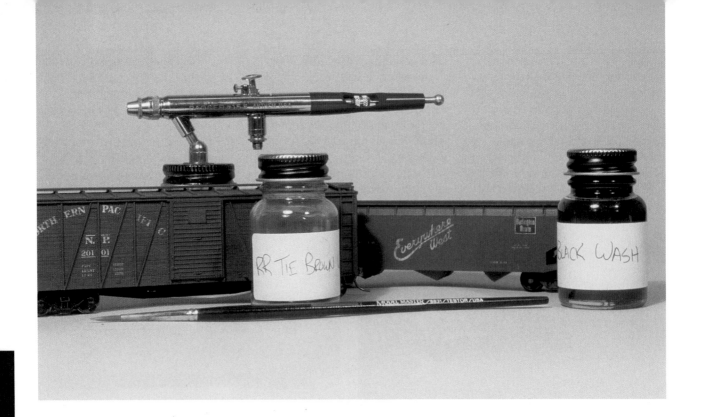

FIVE

Weathering with paint

Using paint to create realistic effects

Now that you have a realistic model with a good-looking paint job and realistic lettering, what's the next step? Although some are loath to dirty up a nice, new-looking model, a good job of weathering will enhance the appearance, bring out details, and make a model much more realistic.

Weathering doesn't mean making every model look like it's weather-beaten and ready to collapse. In fact, usually it's the subtle, light weathering touches that are the most stunning and realistic.

There are many techniques for weathering freight cars, locomotives, structures, and other items. There is no one "right" way to weather, just as everything in real life doesn't age in the same way.

It's a good idea to learn many different methods of weathering. Then, when you're looking at a real freight car or locomotive, you can try to figure out the best method or combination of methods to re-create the prototype effect.

We'll start by looking at several weathering methods using paint.

DRYBRUSHING

Drybrushing is a simple technique that requires no tools fancier than a beat-up, stiff paintbrush. It's a good method for re-creating a streaked look, such as rust stains and peeling paint effects, like those on the prototype boxcar in fig. 5-1.

Drybrushing is hard on brushes, so don't use your nice new brushes for this method. Instead, use either older brushes or—since a stiffer brush usually works better than a soft one—hog-bristle brushes, which are stiff, inexpensive, and quite durable.

Start by dipping just the tip of the bristles in the paint. Brush off most of the paint on a paper towel, as fig. 5-2 shows. Stroke the nearly dry brush on the model, as in fig. 5-3. The results are shown in fig. 5-4.

Among the best uses for drybrushing is to create the look of peeling or streaked lettering and rust. This can be done either lightly and subtly, as on the SP&S boxcar, or more heavily, as on the Burlington hopper car in fig. 5-5.

Other good uses for drybrushing are streaks of rust, exhaust stains, and spilled loads. Chapters 7 and 8 show other examples of how to use drybrushing on models.

The sidebar on page 47 lists many good weathering colors.

Fig. 5-1. Many weathered freight cars take on a streaked appearance.

Fig. 5-2. Dip the tips of the bristles in the paint, then brush off most of the paint on a paper towel.

Fig. 5-3. Stroke the nearly dry brush on the model–in this case, over the lettering.

Fig. 5-4. The final results can be quite subtle, as on this SP&S boxcar.

Fig. 5-5. Drybrushing effects can also be quite heavy.

WASHES

Washes are another quick and easy way of weathering models. They're good for duplicating an overall grungy look, especially on cars with a lot of texture (ribs, wood grain, bracing, and such), such as the real boxcar in fig. 5-6.

Start by making thin washes of paint. I like to use Polly Scale paints, mixed about one part paint to about ten parts Polly S Airbrush Thinner. You can also make acrylic paint washes using water as thinner, but the airbrush thinner has less surface tension than water and will tend to flow more smoothly onto the model surface.

Use as wide a brush as practical.

Brush the wash onto the model, keeping your brush strokes in the direction of the body features. See fig. 5-7. The wash will tend to cling around details such as rivets, ribs, and door details. Figure 5-8 shows the car side after the wash has dried.

Although washes work well on grooved or other rough, irregular surfaces, results can be spotty on smoother surfaces, as fig. 5-9 shows. On a smooth surface it's more likely that you'll be able to see brush strokes or other marks that detract from the overall effect.

If you apply a wash and don't like the effect, you can usually remove it by immediately getting the model under warm running water and scrubbing with a soft-bristled toothbrush. If the wash has a chance to dry, this will be very difficult to do.

Washes can be built up in layers, so remember that you'll have more control over the final results if you apply two or three light coats instead of a single heavy wash.

When you mix paints very thin (such as for washes and sprays), mix only what you plan to use in a couple days' time. After that time, some paint will tend to separate and not mix thoroughly.

Fig. 5-6. Weathering tends to gather around details such as bracing, gaps between boards, rivets, and other raised items, as on this old Burlington wood boxcar.

Fig. 5-7. Brush the wash onto the car–in this case an Accurail boxcar–making sure all areas are covered.

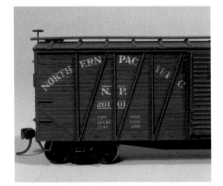

Fig. 5-8. The wash color highlights cracks and other recessed areas and is also pronounced around rivets and other raised details.

Fig. 5-9. Wash effects can be blotchy on smooth surfaces, such as this InterMountain steel refrigerator car.

WEATHERING SPRAYS

If you have an airbrush, thinned paint mixes are an excellent way to create many weathering effects. Mix paint in the same way as for a wash: one part paint to about nine parts thinner.

Among the most common—and effective—uses of a weathering spray are for locomotive exhaust stains (see Chapter 8 for several examples) and for overall grungy effects on both locomotives and freight cars. The prototype car in fig. 5-10 is one example, and fig. 5-11 shows a model car after receiving a grungy spray.

Thinned rust colors can be sprayed on trucks, couplers, and other areas. Thinned earth-tone colors create dust effects on trucks, underframes, and the lower sides of locomotives and freight cars.

Another effective use is to fade lettering. To do this, airbrush a thinned mix of the freight car color over the lettering in thin coats until you achieve the desired effect.

Weathering sprays work well over other weathering effects, such as drybrushing, washes, and chalks.

You can also use oversprays to fade paint. A thinned mix of white, antique white, or light gray, sprayed over the surface, will lighten paint and make it look as if it's fading. Once again, airbrush the mix in thin coats to build up the effect you're looking for.

If you don't own an airbrush, you can get a dust overspray effect by using Floquil's no. 130016 Instant Weathering spray (fig. 5-12). This is a thin dust-colored paint. Be aware that it comes out of the can very quickly; so use care when applying it.

Fig. 5-10. Some old cars have an overall grimy cast that makes it difficult to even read the lettering.

Fig. 5-11. A weathering spray of grimy black or mixed black and grimy black works well for creating an overall grungy look on a model.

Fig. 5-12. Floquil's Instant Weathering spray can be used for dust effects.

OIL COLOR WEATHERING

You can use artist's oil colors to create many weathering effects. They are especially effective at re-creating rust patches and streaks often found on older freight cars like the Cotton Belt boxcar in fig. 5-13.

The three basic colors you'll need are burnt umber, burnt sienna, and raw umber. Squeeze a bit of each color onto a piece of scrap plastic, as fig. 5-14 shows. Use a toothpick to mix a bit of each color together, which gives you a good variety of colors.

Use a fine brush to paint patches of rust on the model (I used an HO Model Die Casting boxcar), using burnt sienna and burnt umber for the darker areas. See fig. 5-15. Raw umber works well for large streaks of lighter rust, or for areas where mother nature has washed rust colors over the paint and lettering, as in fig. 5-16.

Once you have the rust patches where you want them, take a wide flat brush wet with mineral spirits. Stroke the brush downward to further wash the rust color down the car side. See fig. 5-17. This effect can be repeated to make the effect as subtle or strong as you desire. Figure 5-18 shows the finished car side.

Oil paints take quite awhile to dry (a day or two, depending upon how heavily they're applied). This makes it easy to undo effects that don't turn out the way you'd like. Simply take a small cloth with mineral spirits, wipe off the paint, and start over.

Be sure the oil paints are fully dry before adding a flat finish or any other weathering effects with paints or chalks.

Fig. 5-13. Some older freight cars, like this Cotton Belt boxcar, have numerous rust spots where paint and lettering have completely worn away.

Fig. 5-14. Squeeze burnt umber, burnt sienna, and raw umber onto a scrap piece of plastic. Blend them together with a toothpick to give a wide variety of colors.

Fig. 5-15. The darker colors work well for painting small and large rust patches on the model.

Fig. 5-16. Raw umber works well for making streaks of light rust.

Fig. 5-18. The oil paint rust effects are in place. Additional paint or chalk weathering can also be applied.

Fig. 5-17. Stroking a brush damp with mineral spirits down the sides accentuates the streaked effects of the rust colors.

PUTTING IT TOGETHER

Each of the above techniques is quite useful in re-creating different weathering effects. The next chapter looks at chalks and other materials that can be used for weathering, and Chapters 7 and 8 show how to combine these methods to capture various looks on freight cars and locomotives.

Weathering colors

Good colors to simulate **rust** include Polly Scale 414323 Rust (for new rust), 414275 Roof Brown, 414329, and Railroad Tie Brown, and Badger Modelflex 16172 Rust, 16175 Rail Brown, and 16176 Roof Brown.

Good colors for **exhaust and general grime** are Polly Scale 110010 Engine Black and 110013 Grimy Black and Modelflex 1603 Grimy Black and 16119 Flat Black.

If you're looking for an oily color, such as a **fuel spill or stain,** try Polly Scale 414326 Oily Black.

Colors for **general dust and dirt** effects include Polly Scale 110081 Earth, 110083 Mud, and 110086 Grime, and Modelflex 16174 Earth.

Along with the above paints, there are many other colors that will work as well. Don't worry too much about the name of the paint—look at the color.

Weathering with chalks

Creating alternative weathering effects

Chalks are an inexpensive, easy-to-use material that can be used to re-create many weathering effects on freight cars, locomotives, structures, streets, and other details. With a bit of practice you'll find it relatively easy to get good-looking, consistent results with chalks. However, there are a few important keys to obtaining realistic results.

SIX

First, use only good-quality artist's pastel chalks, as shown in fig. 6-1. Avoid kids' playground chalk and packages of cheap chalkboard chalk. They will sometimes provide good results, but sometimes not.

Two types of chalk are shown in fig. 6-1. Common artist's pastels are relatively inexpensive, work well, and are large enough to yield enough weathering material to last for a long time.

Artist's oil pastels are smaller and slightly more expensive. They have an oil base that makes them less powdery, and they cling to surfaces better than regular pastels.

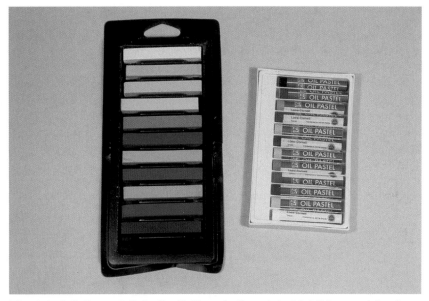

Fig. 6-1. Artist's pastel chalks (left) and oil pastels (right) in several colors are handy for weathering. Both of these sets are from Loew-Cornell.

PREPARATION

The first step in weathering with chalks is to make sure that the surface to be weathered has a dead-flat sheen. Chalks need a surface with some "tooth" to grab onto. It is nearly impossible to get chalks to stay put on a gloss finish, and even a semi-gloss surface can be difficult to work with.

Because of this, a good first step is to spray the model with a light coat of clear flat. My favorite is Polly Scale clear flat finish applied with an airbrush; my second choice, if you don't have an airbrush, is Model Master Clear Flat from a spray can.

It's easiest to work with chalks in powdered form. Scrape chalk with the edge of a hobby knife to get a supply of powder, as fig. 6-2 shows. I use old film canisters to store the powdered chalk, but other small containers will work as well.

I prefer hog-bristle brushes for applying chalks, as they're fairly stiff (not to mention quite inexpensive). I keep an assortment (large and small, flat and round) of brushes handy and use them strictly for chalks. Softer brushes can also work well—try a few and stick with what gives you the best results.

Apply the chalks to the model

surface, as shown in fig. 6-3. Start by dipping the bristles into the powdered chalk. Brush the chalk using quick swipes of the brush. As with other types of weathering, it's best to start light and add more chalk later if needed.

If you get too much chalk on the surface, you can brush much of it off with a clean, stiff brush, or you can wash off the chalk with water and start over.

Oil pastels take a bit of a different approach. Scraping them with a knife won't yield a powder—instead, the oil base makes the chalk clumpy. I find it easiest to

Fig. 6-2. Use a knife to scrape pastel chalks to get powder for weathering.

Fig. 6-3. Apply the chalk to the model with top-to-bottom strokes. Here black chalk is applied to a yellow Walthers refrigerator car.

rub the chalk against a piece of coarse sandpaper, as in fig. 6-4, and then rub the brush into the sandpaper to pick up the chalk. You can also rub the brush directly against the chalk.

Either way, the process of applying the chalks is the same as regular pastels, but it tends to go more slowly. See fig. 6-5. It generally takes more applications with the oil pastels, but the colors can be darker

and more pronounced. It's a good idea to practice on a scrap shell or old freight car body to get the techniques down.

Several colors of chalk are handy. Black chalk works well for exhaust stains and general grime, and you can mix black and white powder to make various shades of gray.

Browns and oranges can be used (and mixed) to create rust effects, and earth tones work well

for a general dusty appearance.

Remember to keep your brush strokes in the direction that real-life weathering effects travel—usually downward on freight cars and locomotives. If you want a general dusted appearance—such as around exhaust stacks—dab the brush straight to the surface repeatedly without stroking it.

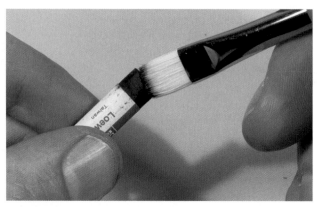

Fig. 6-4. With oil pastels you can either grind the chalk on sandpaper (above) or rub a stiff brush directly against the chalk (above right).

Fig. 6-5. Applying oil pastels is much the same as using regular pastels, but the process goes more slowly.

SEALING THE WEATHERING

To keep from smearing chalk weathering, it's important to seal it with a coat of clear finish. In the past this has been the downfall of chalk weathering—chalks have a reputation for disappearing when a clear coat is applied.

However, using quality chalks and applying them to a flat surface as described above, then following with a light coat or two of clear fin-ish should eliminate that problem.

Figure 6-6 shows the Armour refrigerator car after being coated by my favorite clear flat finish, Polly Scale clear flat. You can see that both the regular pastels (left side of the car) and oil pastels (right side) held up well to two light coats of clear flat.

The blue Walthers reefer in fig. 6-7 also received regular pastel weathering on the left and oil pas-tels on the right. This car is shown after receiving a coat of Model Master clear semi-gloss lacquer from a spray can. Once again, the chalks held up well to the lacquer clearcoat.

If you still have problems with pastel colors disappearing (or being toned down) after spraying, then stick with oil pastels.

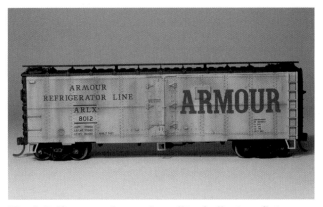

Fig. 6-6. If you apply good-quality chalks to a flat finish, the chalks will hold up well even after receiving a sealing spray of clear flat finish.

Fig. 6-7. This Walthers refrigerator car received a spray of Model Master clear semi-gloss from a spray can. The chalks have held up well to the spray.

CRAYONS

Artist's crayons (fig. 6-8) can also be very effective weathering tools. They're available in a wide range of colors. I keep black (exhaust and grime), light and dark brown (rust), white (chalky lettering), and gray (grime) crayons handy.

Use a knife to sharpen each crayon to a point, as in fig. 6-9. It can then be used to streak or high-light details on a model, as fig. 6-10 shows. They are especially effec-tive for highlighting raised details. After applying them, you can rub them with a finger or soft cloth to soften the effect.

Crayons, pastels, and oil pastels can all be found at arts and crafts supply stores and at some hobby shops as well.

Now that we've reviewed the various weathering methods with chalks and paint, let's look at how to combine all of these tech-niques to re-create effects found in real life.

Fig. 6-8. Artist's crayons are available in a variety of colors.

Fig. 6-9. Use a knife to whittle a point on the crayon.

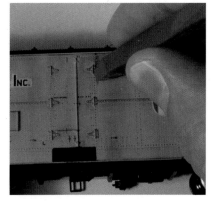

Fig. 6-10. Hold the crayons like a small pencil, applying the color directly to the model or detail.

Weathering freight cars

Exploring subtle techniques that make a big difference

Once a prototype freight car rolls out of the factory, dust, grime, and exhaust residue begin accumulating, scratches and dents begin occurring, and in many cases, rust begins to form. Over the years old lettering is painted out, new lettering is stenciled in, and minor repairs are made.

The end result is that after several years on the road the average freight car starts to look pretty beat up. Whereas locomotives receive frequent service, repaintings, and—on many railroads—regular cleaning, the typical freight car survives 15 or 20 years without so much as a washing.

All of this combines to make the ubiquitous freight car the ideal starting point for weathering and upgrading. We'll look at a few tricks that can be done on any freight car, with methods that can be used to enhance factory-painted cars as well as those you've painted and lettered yourself.

SEVEN

WHEELS AND TRUCKS

Let's start at the bottom, where grime and rust often show their first signs. Freight car trucks are of two basic types: solid-bearing (sometimes incorrectly called friction-bearing) and roller-bearing.

Solid-bearing trucks were identified by having journal boxes at each axle end. See fig. 7-1. The journal boxes held cotton waste soaked in oil to lubricate the friction points.

In the 1960s roller-bearing trucks gained in popularity. These trucks were free-rolling and didn't require the constant lubricating of solid-bearing trucks. They have round caps at the axle ends, which rotate as the wheel turns. See fig. 7-2. All cars in interchange service since 1980 are required to have roller-bearing trucks.

It's important to know the difference in truck types, because wheels on each type of truck tend to weather differently. Wheel faces on solid-bearing trucks tend to accumulate a layer of dark, oily residue from the journal-box oil. Wheel faces on roller-bearing trucks don't get this. Instead they tend to take on an overall rusty color, which can range from a bright orange to dark brown.

Figure 7-3 shows how to paint model wheelsets. Just use a medium brush and the appropriate color paint. Virtually any rust color will work for wheels on roller-bearing trucks.

For wheels in solid-bearing trucks, start with black or grimy black. To get the greasy appearance of the real wheels, try Polly Scale Oily Black, which dries with a

Fig. 7-1. Solid-bearing trucks can be identified by their journal-box covers (this is a Barber-Bettendorf truck with leaf springs). Note the rust colors on the truck sideframes and the oily appearance of the wheel faces.

Fig. 7-2. Roller-bearing trucks, used on all modern equipment, have rotating axle ends. Note the rust colors on the wheel faces.

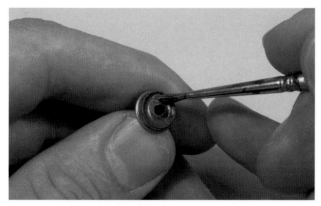

Fig. 7-3. Rotate the wheelset between your fingers as you hold the brush to the wheel face.

Fig. 7-4. You can use a variety of black and rust colors to paint truck sideframes.

realistic oily appearance. Make sure you don't get paint onto the wheel treads themselves.

New trucks are generally painted either the car color or black (wheels are unpainted), but they weather fairly quickly to various shades of grimy black and brown.

For painting trucks, start with a palette of several colors, as fig. 7-4 shows, including black, grimy black, and several browns. Use a brush to paint trucks with combinations of colors. The older the car, the more varied the colors can be.

On roller-bearing trucks the roller-bearing adapter (the small fitting directly over the roller-bearing axle end) is usually a shade of dark red. Paint this with a boxcar red color, and highlight the bolts on the roller-bearing end caps with a dark or medium gray. Figure 7-5 shows completed trucks.

Fig. 7-5. Note the variations in the wheel face and truck sideframe colors on the completed solid-bearing (left) and roller-bearing (right) trucks.

ROOFS

Let's move from the bottom to the top. Roofs are important on freight car models, since we spend a lot of time looking down at our layouts.

Modern boxcar roofs are typically unpainted galvanized steel. This has a metallic sheen, but it is dull and not the shiny silver color found on many commercial models. See fig. 7-6. In addition, most boxcars have an overspray of the car color along the roof edges.

If you have a painted car that should have a galvanized roof, start by painting it flat silver, as fig. 7-7 shows. You can use a brush, airbrush, or spray can for this.

To give the silver roof a galvanized look, give it an overspray of thinned grimy black paint (about one part paint to nine parts thinner). Apply just enough to kill the silver shine. The result will be a dull gray roof with a metallic sheen. Finish the roof with a light thinned spray of the car color around the edges, as in fig. 7-8. This doesn't have to be an exact match to provide a good effect.

As these roofs weather, the galvanized coating tends to wear off over time. This results in light and dark patches of rust, as fig. 7-6 shows. Duplicate this on a model by brushing dark and light browns on the roof, as in fig. 7-9. This effect is most often seen directly above the door openings, where hasty forklift drivers raise their loads prematurely, denting and damaging the roof.

Older boxcar roofs often had their galvanized roofs painted over with the body color. Over time the paint would wear off the galvanized areas. You can simulate this on a model as fig. 7-10 shows, by painting streaks of flat silver in varied patterns across the roof.

Fig. 7-6. Boxcar roofs are often galvanized steel, a dull metallic gray color. Note the overspray of the yellow body color around the edges of the roof. Also note the rust on the trailing boxcar roof.

Fig. 7-7. To model a galvanized roof, start by brush-painting or airbrushing the roof flat silver (this is Polly Scale Flat Aluminum).

Some roofs should have just a bit of silver showing; others should have a lot. Finish the roof with a grimy black overspray as you did on the modern boxcar roofs.

The tops of covered hoppers also pose some interesting weathering possibilities. Note the photo of the prototype covered hopper in fig. 7-11. Of its four roof hatches, only one is original—the others have all been replaced over time.

This is easy to simulate on a model, as fig. 7-12 shows. The hatches are separate pieces in the InterMountain car in the photo (and two styles were included with the kit), so it was easy to paint one a different color and add it to the car.

On cars where the hatches are a single casting you can get a similar effect by painting one or more of the hatches a different color.

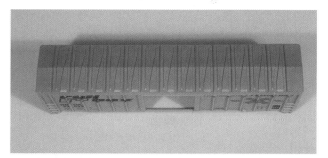

Fig. 7-8. Tone down the silver color with a light spray of thinned grimy black. A thinned mix of yellow around the edges simulates the overspray found on prototype roofs.

Fig. 7-9. Paint areas of dark and light browns to simulate the rust colors found on many prototype roofs.

Fig. 7-10. Silver patches on older boxcars simulate where paint has worn off the galvanized metal. Give the roofs a coat of thinned grimy black to dull the silver.

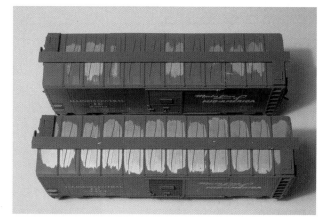

Fig. 7-11. Hatches on covered hoppers are often damaged and replaced, often with little thought to color or style. The spilled grain around the hatches would be interesting to model.

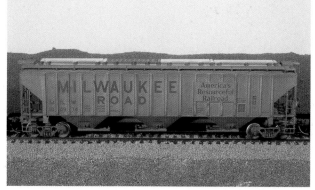

Fig. 7-12. This InterMountain hopper included two styles of hatches, so it was easy to paint a few a different color before installing them.

TANK CARS

Chemical stains and load spills often give prototype tank cars an interesting appearance. Look at prototype cars and photos and figure out the best ways to re-create the effects on a model. An example is the molten sulfur car in fig. 7-13.

I simulated the sulfur load by mixing some greenish-yellow paint and streaking it on the model, followed by some black streaks to simulate where the dried sulfur had peeled off.

The sulfur car in fig. 7-13 has stenciling indicating its lading, which is common for cars in dedicated service. I added this to the model using small dry-transfer lettering sets. This isn't as tedious as it looks and adds a great deal to the cars' appearance.

Fig. 7-13. Streaks and splatters of yellow-green paint help this Walthers HO model match the prototype molten sulfur tank car.

CHALKY LETTERING

On many older cars the lettering paint has begun to oxidize, with mother nature streaking it down the sides of the car. The Southern boxcar in fig. 7-14 is one example.

One way of simulating this is with a white artist's crayon, as fig. 7-15 shows. Start by tracing over the bottom of the letters with the crayon. Follow this by using a brush to stroke down the sides of the car. This captures the streaked appearance of the real thing.

Fig. 7-14. Lettering on prototype cars, such as this Southern boxcar, sometimes gets chalky and runs down the sides of the car.

Fig. 7-15. Go over the lower parts of the letters with a white artist's crayon, then use a stiff brush to streak the crayon down the car side. The car is a factory-painted Accurail boxcar.

CHANGING CAR NUMBERS

A common problem in building a freight car fleet with factory-painted cars is that you can easily wind up with several cars with the same road number.

It's possible to remove factory-painted numbers and add new ones. Figure 7-16 shows one method using a common pencil eraser. Start rubbing the eraser across the numbers until they begin to disappear. Depending upon the ink and paint used, the numbers may come off easily, or—as on this Accurail car—the paint

will come off before the letters disappear.

If this happens, don't worry. Find a paint that's close to the body color, testing the paint on a hidden spot on the car, as fig. 7-17 shows. Once you find paint that's close, touch up the body as needed, as in fig. 7-18.

Add new decal numerals, as in fig. 7-19. These can come from a lettering set for that paint scheme, or from an alphabet set that's close to the original lettering style.

It's tempting to change just one

or two numerals instead of the whole number, but it's actually easier—and the final effect will be better—if you change the whole car number.

This technique also works for changing other lettering as well. I wanted to backdate the Illinois Central refrigerator car in fig. 7-20 with the earlier diamond logo instead of the rail logo that was on the car. I used a pencil eraser again, and this time the lettering came off easily without removing any paint.

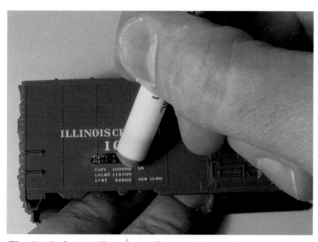

Fig. 7-16. A pencil eraser often works well to remove factory-applied lettering, although sometimes it will take paint off as well (as on this Accurail car).

Fig. 7-17. Test potential paint matches on hidden areas of the shell.

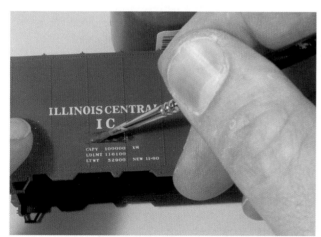

Fig. 7-18. Touch up the area where the eraser removed the factory paint.

Fig. 7-19. Add the new decal weathering over the touched-up area.

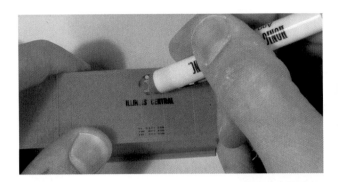
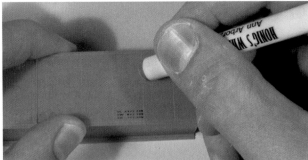

Fig. 7-20. The eraser removed the IC rail herald from this Inter-Mountain car without removing any paint. The diamond herald is from a Microscale decal set.

PAINT TOUCHUP

In the past few years factory paint jobs from most manufacturers have become much better in both quality and prototype fidelity. Paint jobs now often include many detail items, such as consolidated stencils, ACI labels, and small detail lettering (see the sidebar on page 61 for a summary of freight car lettering).

Fig. 7-21. Use a brush to touch up unpainted brake wheels and other details to match the body color. This is a Model Die Casting hopper car.

There's often room for additional details, especially when updating a car that's supposedly been in service for 10 or 15 years.

Figure 7-21 shows a basic change that should be made on many older Athearn and Roundhouse cars. The brakewheels on many of these older cars are simply molded in black instead of matching the car color. Painting them to match the body makes them blend in much better.

Sometimes the lettering needs to be touched up a bit, especially on cars with pronounced ribs. Figure 7-22 shows how to close any gaps in the lettering using a fine-point brush. The appearance is dramatically improved.

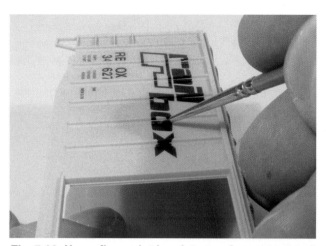 

Fig. 7-22. Use a fine-point brush to touch up any gaps in lettering along ribs and braces.

DECAL DETAILING

Microscale, Champion, and other decal manufacturers offer decals for detail items such as consolidated stencils, ACI plates, wheel inspection dots, and manufacturer's initials and logos. (See the sidebar on page 61 for information on when these details appeared on real cars.) Figure 7-23 shows a few of them.

I decided to dress up an Accurail covered hopper to match a prototype Great Northern car that I had photographed in the early 1990s. See fig. 7-24.

Start by trimming the consoli-dated stencil from Champ set no. HD-32. Apply it like any other decal (fig. 7-25), then finish the decaling with an ACI plate from Microscale set no. 87-2.

The load limit and light weight on the real car had been restenciled. To capture this look, prior to weathering the car, place a piece of masking tape over this data, as fig. 7-26 shows. Once the weathering is complete, removing the tape will make it look as if the area has been repainted and restenciled.

I used a mix of drybrushing and a thinned grimy black overspray to weather the car. To keep the dry-brush effects where I wanted them (namely, over the weld seams) I made a template from a piece of .010″ styrene, as fig. 7-27 shows.

As this project shows, getting realistic results is a matter of looking at a prototype car and figuring out the best methods of duplicating the effects on a model.

Fig. 7-23. Decal details include Microscale ACI plates and boxcar lettering (left) and Champ sets for wheel inspection dots, consolidated stencils, and manufacturer's logos.

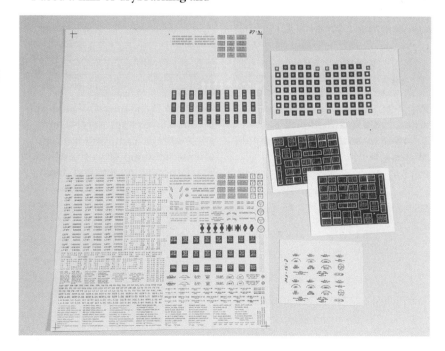

Fig. 7-24. The prototype Great Northern car was photographed in 1991, more than 20 years after the Burlington Northern merger. The model started as a factory-painted Accurail covered hopper.

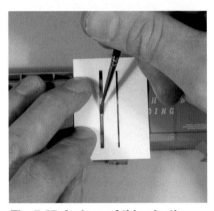

Fig. 7-25. Add the consolidated stencil from the Champion set, followed by the ACI plate from the Microscale set.

Fig. 7-26. Place masking tape over the load limit, light weight, and shop initials. Removing the tape after weathering gives the effect of repainted and restenciled data.

Fig. 7-27. A piece of thin plastic with slits works well to guide drybrushing, in this case over the car's weld seams.

Freight car lettering and markings

There's a wide variety of lettering and markings on freight cars, and knowing what each item means can help you make more accurate and more realistic models. Here's a summary of what it all means:

1. Road name and herald: This can be as simple as a small herald or as complex as a slogan or full road name (or combination). This lettering is optional, and some modern cars don't carry either a road name or a herald.

2. Reporting marks: Each owner is assigned a unique set of identifying initials. Marks that end in "X" indicate privately owned cars.

3. Number: The car's identifying number. Each car number is unique to its owner.

4. Capacity: The car's designed capacity in pounds. This appeared on new cars through 1985, but since then this lettering hasn't been required. This was to have been painted out on older cars by January 1993, but it can still be found on many cars into the new century.

5. Load limit: The maximum weight for the load itself.

6. Light weight: The car's weight when empty. If the word "NEW" appears, the weight was taken when the car was built, with the built date stenciled alongside. When a car is reweighed (usually after repairs), the new weight is stenciled here, along with the initials of the shop and the date of the reweighing.

7. Car type: The AAR car designation. On this car it is RBL, which is an insulated boxcar (XM is a plain boxcar, and other cars have their own designations).

8. Plate clearance: Cars are assigned plate designations based on their length, width, and height. This is a Plate C boxcar, meaning that it can safely travel on most routes. Larger cars (Plates D, E, etc.) are limited by bridge, tunnel, and other clearances.

9. Tack and route boards: These are used to tack cards regarding the car's lading or loading/unloading instructions (large board) or route (small board).

10. Built date: The date the car was built. On newer cars this appears only in the consolidated stencil.

11. Dimensions: The inside and outside measurements of the car. Covered hoppers (and some boxcars) include capacity in cubic feet; tank cars have capacity in gallons; and ice-bunker refrigerator cars include ice capacity in pounds.

12. Consolidated stencils: These began appearing in 1974. Early cars had single panels; modern cars have two or three panels. The panels include dates and initials of shops performing brake and other work on the car.

13. ACI (Automatic Car Identification) plate: ACI, an optical identification system, used trackside scanners to read colored panels on cars. The system first appeared in 1967, with all cars required to have ACI plates by 1970. The system never worked well (grime was the main problem), and in 1977 the requirement was eliminated. Cars built or repainted after 1977 won't have them, but older cars can still be found with old ACI plates into the new century.

14. Wheel inspection dots: These began appearing in March 1978 when U-1 wheels (made by a certain manufacturer) were found to be defective. All cars of 70-ton or less capacity with 33" wheels were required to be inspected. Those found to be without U-1 wheels were given a black square with yellow dot; those with U-1 wheels got a white dot. All U-1 wheels had to be replaced by December 1978. Cars new or repainted in 1979 and later won't have this mark.

Other car lettering includes builder's insignia; specifications of truck, wheel, and brake equipment; and stenciling regarding load restrictions.

Graffiti

Few things in the world of weathering are as controversial as graffiti. Until the 1970s graffiti usually consisted of scrawled notes and messages, everything from "Kilroy was here" to "Class of 72." Today graffiti is often large, elaborate, and multicolored, and a lot of it finds its way onto freight cars and other railroad items.

Even if you can't stand the sight of it, graffiti is part of today's landscape. If you choose not to model it, that's certainly okay, but if you choose to model it, take the time to make it realistic.

Probably the easiest way to add graffiti is with decals. Both Microscale and Blair Line offer several sets of modern tag-style graffiti decals, and Microscale and others offer older-style scrawled markings. They can be applied to a model just like any other decal.

A good effect is to weather the car prior to adding the decal. This makes it look as if the car spent some time (several years, perhaps) on the road before receiving its graffiti. You can also weather over some graffiti, but make other graffiti appear new.

If you want to create your own, the best way I've found is by using gel pens. These are similar to regular pens, but the ink is thicker (almost like paint). Buy a set that includes white, black, and several colors. The pens will write well on most flat-finish surfaces, so if a car has a gloss or semi-gloss finish, give it a coat of clear flat before using gel pens on it.

The white pen is very handy, since it can be used to simulate common chalk marks as well as graffiti. You can use other colors to produce fancy graffiti or effects. Be sure one color is completely dry before adding the second (the gel ink can take several minutes to dry), or you'll smear the first color.

Gel pens work best over fairly even surfaces, but with some practice you can apply them over small surface details. To get around large details (such as boxcar or hopper car ribs) you can use a fine-point brush to add a bit of ink in the crevices where the pen tip won't reach.

Gel pens can also be used to create other effects, such as handmade signs.

Microscale and Blair Line offer graffiti decals that can be applied to a model just like any other decal.

Gel pens offer an easy way to create unique graffiti.

A white pen is handy, since it can be used to simulate chalk marks as well as graffiti.

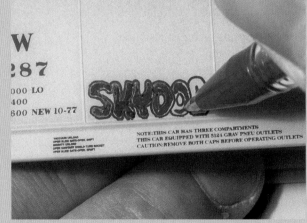

You can use multiple colors to produce fancy graffiti or effects.

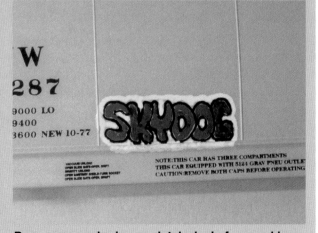

Be sure one color is completely dry before working with another.

Weathering locomotives

Re-creating effects from prototype diesel and steam engines

Like freight cars, model locomotives have improved greatly in quality and detailing in recent years, but there are still many things you can do to improve the appearance of stock locomotives. Of course, you can also use these tricks on models you've painted yourself.

Let's start by going step-by-step through upgrading a factory-painted diesel. I started with a Life-Like Proto 2000 SD7, but you can apply these techniques to other locomotives.

EIGHT

CB&Q SD7

I started with a stock HO scale Life-Like Proto 2000 for this project. Figure 8-1 shows how I tried to make the model appear as if it had been in service for a while, like the prototype locomotive in the photo.

Figure 8-2 shows that this model is sharp right from the box, with a good-looking paint scheme and lots of separately applied detail parts. One challenge with many factory-painted locomotives is that with all the prototype variations (headlights, horns, pilots, and the like) an individual model might not have all the details to match the specific prototype.

The first thing I did to this model was add a Burlington-style headlight casting (Sunrise no. H-101) on each end. Figure 8-3 shows how the molded headlight casting had to be removed before the new casting could be glued in place.

The new casting was a metal part, so it had to be painted to match the locomotive. As Chapter 1 explained, this is among the most difficult painting tasks, since there's no magic formula to matching paint.

I finally found a mix close enough for my eye and painted the castings, as in fig. 8-4. A bit of tape on a piece of cardstock makes a handy painting handle for detail parts. Glue the castings in place with CA (cyanoacrylate adhesive). I also added a new steam generator stack on the short hood (Details West no. 118), which is taller (like the real CB&Q stack) than the factory part.

Fig. 8-1. This Chicago, Burlington & Quincy locomotive is in fairly good shape, but many obvious signs show that it has been in service for a while. Weathering the Life-Like model makes it much more realistic.

Fig. 8-2. Here's how the Life-Like model looked right out of the box.

WEATHERING LOCOMOTIVES

Grills on locomotives—especially in light-colored areas as on this SD7—lack an appearance of depth. Fix this by adding a wash of black or grimy black paint to all grill areas, as fig. 8-5 shows. I also added a black wash to the louver areas where the lettering falls on the long hood. You can see the difference in comparing photos of the new and finished models.

Moving to the roof, paint the insides of the exhaust stacks flat black. See fig. 8-6. Use chalks or a thinned spray of grimy black to add exhaust stains around the stacks, as in fig. 8-7. Drybrush or use chalks to streak the top of the cab roof as well (note how the prototype cab roof appears in fig. 8-1).

Finish the roof weathering by using a brown artist's crayon to make rust streaks on the outsides of the exhaust stacks, as in fig. 8-8, and adding some grime around the steam generator details on the short hood. Give the shell a coat of Polly Scale Clear Flat to seal the weathering.

Whether you prefer a flat or semi-gloss finish on your locomotives, remember that a few areas, such as windows and windshields, shouldn't have this flat finish. Paint these with

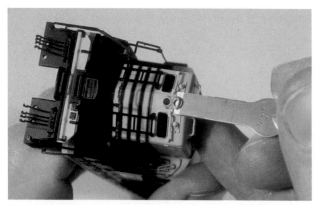
Fig. 8-3. The cast-on headlights had to be removed with a hobby knife to make way for the new castings.

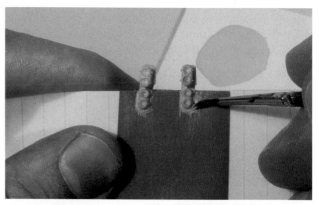
Fig. 8-4. A piece of card and some tape made a handy painting handle for the new headlight castings.

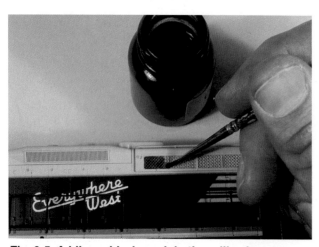
Fig. 8-5. Adding a black wash in the grills gives an appearance of depth.

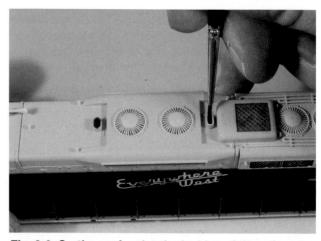
Fig. 8-6. On the roof, paint the insides of the exhaust stacks flat black.

clear gloss to restore the shine, as fig. 8-9 shows.

Move under the locomotive to the tanks. On the steam-generator-equipped locomotive the model is patterned upon, the lead tank was for water and the rear tank for fuel. Start by brush-painting the tanks with grimy black (or a flat black-grimy black mix), as in fig. 8-10. Any brush marks will look like grime that has washed down the sides.

Make a fuel spill coming down from the fuel filler with Polly Scale Oily Black. You can also add other rusty and grimy streaks to the tank with chalks or drybrushing.

I airbrushed the trucks with thinned mixes of grimy black and brown, as fig. 8-11 shows. You could also get the same effects with chalks.

Most locomotive trucks have parts that aren't meant to be seen, including brass and bronze electrical contacts and shiny metal or plastic truck towers. Use a brush and flat black paint to cover these areas, as in fig. 8-12.

The finished locomotive, shown in fig. 8-1, is not heavily weathered. However, the weathering that's there highlights details and makes it look like an engine that's been in service.

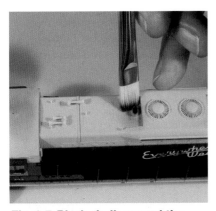

Fig. 8-7. Black chalk around the stacks works well for simulating exhaust soot.

Fig. 8-8. A brown artist's crayon makes realistic rust streaks outside the stacks.

Fig. 8-9. Clear gloss will restore the shine to windows if they've become grimy.

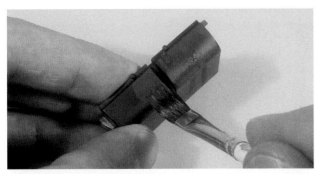

Fig. 8-10. Brush-paint the tank casting with grimy black (left), then add a simulated fuel spill with Polly Scale Oily Black (right).

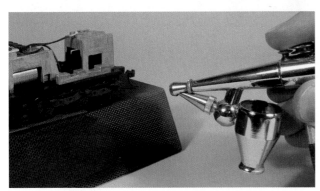

Fig. 8-11. Airbrush the trucks with grimy black and dark rust colors.

Fig. 8-12. Use flat black to hide any areas that should not be seen, such as the brass electrical contact strips.

FAN DETAILS AND BLACK DIESELS

Many locomotives with cast-in-place details have fans molded with blade detail. However, even if the molding quality is good, the detail is hard to see when everything is painted the same color.

You can highlight this by using a fine-point brush to carefully paint the molded fan blades with flat silver paint. Take your time, but don't worry if some paint gets on the grill. See fig. 8-13.

Once that's done and dry, use a brush with some of the roof color to paint the fan grills, touching up any stray silver paint. The result, as

fig. 8-13 shows, is the appearance of fan blades beneath grills. It's not as nice as superdetailed fans with separate blades, but it's a better effect than the factory paint job and a lot less work.

Black diesels can be more difficult to weather than lighter-colored engines—after all, black exhaust stains aren't very effective on black paint. However, as the prototype engine in fig. 8-14 shows, black diesels aren't really black. You can see how this Norfolk Southern engine has weathered with lighter gray areas,

with exhaust stains and other marks visible.

One way of capturing this on a model is to use white or light gray chalk (or a thinned overspray of white or light gray paint) to lighten the roof. Follow this by using black chalks or a black weathering spray to highlight the areas around the exhaust stacks. See fig. 8-15.

Figure 8-16 shows the completed engine next to one straight from the box. Note how the lighter-colored weathering makes the model's details much easier to see.

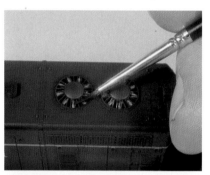

Fig. 8-13. Start by painting the cast-in fan blades silver (above). Painting the fan grills black (above right) makes it look like the blades are below the grills (above, far right).

Fig. 8-14. This Norfolk Southern diesel shows that black diesels aren't necessarily black. The roof has faded to dark gray, but it's stained black around the exhaust stack.

Fig. 8-16. Note the dramatic difference between the weathered locomotive below and the stock black engine at top. The HO models are Atlas GP7s.

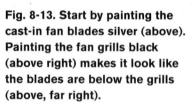

Fig. 8-15. Apply white chalk to lighten the roof, followed by black around the exhaust stacks.

WEATHERING LOCOMOTIVES

F UNIT WEATHERING

The prototype photo in fig. 8-17 shows how F units often kicked up weathering along their sides in what has become known as a "bow-wave" pattern. Note how the grime appears on the sides beginning at the rear of the lead truck, then grows and feathers along the side.

You can create this effect on a model with chalks, as fig. 8-18 shows. Pick a color that matches the real thing, then start dabbing and brushing it on the side of the model. Figure 8-19 shows the finished F unit.

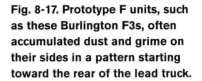

Fig. 8-17. Prototype F units, such as these Burlington F3s, often accumulated dust and grime on their sides in a pattern starting toward the rear of the lead truck.

Fig. 8-18. Brush dust-colored chalk along the sides to match the pattern on the real locomotives.

Fig. 8-19. The finished weathering on the painted Stewart F3 is quite realistic.

NUMBER BOARDS

Many locomotive models in HO and even N scale now come with numbers in their number boards—a great improvement over models of ten years ago. For those that don't include numbers—or those that have them poorly done at the factory—this is one of the easiest improvements you can make to a model, and one that results in dramatic improvement in appearance.

Several styles and types of number board numerals are available from Microscale and ShellScale, as fig. 8-20 shows. Take a good look at the prototype you're trying to model, because real number board numbers come in a variety of styles.

Adding the numerals is a matter of first painting or using a decal to apply a white or black background to the number board. ShellScale

and Microscale both include these (in different sizes and shapes) in their sets, and you can also use Microscale's trim film.

Make sure the base decal is completely dry before adding the numbers. See fig. 8-21. You can see the difference between models with and without numbers in fig. 8-22.

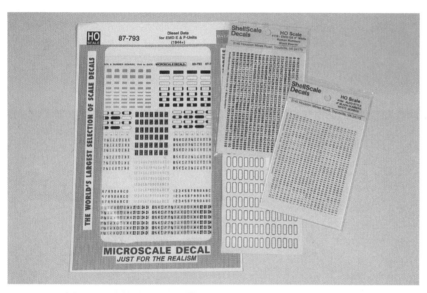

Fig. 8-20. Microscale and ShellScale both offer number board decals in several scales and styles.

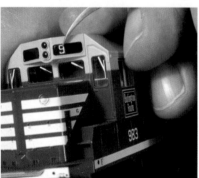

Fig. 8-21. Make sure that the background (in this case black) decal is completely dry before adding the numerals.

Fig. 8-22. Adding numbers in the number boards is one of the most striking improvements you can make to a stock locomotive. The models are HO Kato GP35s.

HANDRAILS

Yet another recent improvement by manufacturers is the inclusion of appropriately colored handrails and stanchions. This is especially welcome since most handrail/stanchion castings are molded in acetal engineering plastic (Delrin is one brand), which is difficult to paint.

Some models still include metal handrails and stanchions (Athearn's standard line and others). These can be easily brush-painted the appropriate color.

Vertical handrails at the corner steps of locomotives are usually painted a bright color to increase visibility. A good paint to use for handrails is Pactra Racing Finish, an extremely flexible paint designed for use on clear R/C car bodies.

Figure 8-23 shows how to apply it to a handrail. When painting engineering plastic, it's important to completely coat the handrail so that the paint forms its own "jacket" around the part. This will

help keep it from scratching off. Two coats are usually necessary for complete coverage.

The Life-Like Great Northern switcher required white on the corner handrails, but don't automatically reach for the white paint—check photos for specific prototype examples. Some railroads used yellow, and others used odd combinations of colors.

Fig. 8-23. Pactra's Racing Finish is a flexible paint that works well on locomotive handrails. Be sure to coat the entire handrail so the paint forms a jacket around the part.

STEAM LOCOMOTIVES

When painting a steam locomotive, start by carefully considering the base color. Although most prototype steam locomotives were black, keep in mind that black is a lousy color for a model. If you're painting a model from scratch, don't paint it black—instead, use a mix of black and grimy black.

Models that are pure black (including diesels—note the Illinois Central Geeps earlier in the chapter) hide details. Painting them a lighter shade, along with adding lighter weathering, enhances the detail and realism.

Start under the locomotive with the running gear and hidden parts. The Mantua locomotive in fig. 8-24

has rods and wheels that are way too shiny. The motor and drive shaft are also quite visible between the running gear and boiler.

Take care of this by painting parts that aren't supposed to be there (the shiny metal motor and the drive shaft) with flat black. You'll still see their outlines, but they will no longer reflect light, hiding them from normal view. See fig. 8-24.

A problem in weathering steam locomotives is that the rods and valve gear are in front of the wheels. If you apply a weathering spray, the rods will act like a mask, keeping the weathering from some areas of the wheels.

A way around this is shown in

fig. 8-25. Place a length of track in your spray booth, hook up two wires from a power pack, and run the locomotive at slow to medium speed while airbrushing the running gear. That's how I weathered both the Mantua Mikado in fig. 8-24 and the brass 4-8-4 in fig. 8-26.

Other weathering on the Burlington locomotive in fig. 8-26 includes black exhaust streaks down each side of the smokebox; exhaust dusting on the stack; light sand-colored streaks on the boiler around the sandbox; and grimy black spray on the smokebox, the firebox sides, and several places on the boiler.

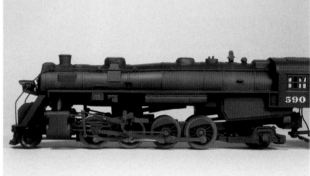

Fig. 8-24. Weathering the running gear and painting parts such as the exposed motor and drive gear improved the realism of this HO scale Mantua steam locomotive.

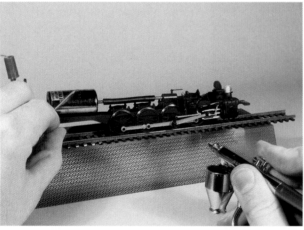

Fig. 8-25. Airbrushing the running gear while the locomotive is running provides even weathering on the wheels, rods, and valve gear.

Fig. 8-26. This painted brass 4-8-4 steam locomotive has drybrushed and airbrushed weathering on the smokebox, boiler, and running gear.

Hiding metal truck towers

Many older locomotive models—notably Athearn's standard line—have truck gear towers with unpainted metal sides. These tend to catch and reflect light, giving models an unrealistic appearance when viewed from low angles.

An easy and quick way to take care of the problem, as the photo shows, is to paint the exposed metal areas flat black. Be sure not to get paint inside the truck tower, and keep paint away from the moving plastic pieces that protrude slightly from the towers.

Paint the wheel faces a flat rust color such as rust, rail brown, or roof brown.

Once the sideframes are back in place, the truck towers all but disappear.

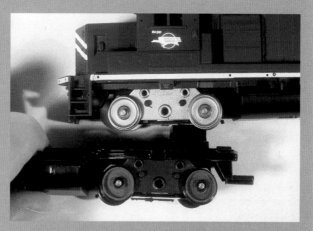

Weathering couplers

Couplers are detail items that require some special treatment on both locomotives and freight cars. Prototype couplers are unpainted (as are wheels, to make it easier to check for flaws), so they tend to be rust-colored.

You can safely airbrush model couplers with thinned mixes of rusty and grimy paints without fear of gumming up the springs or moving parts. Be sure to apply the paints thinned and in thin coats, gradually building them to the effect you're looking for.

Start with a dark brown base color, being sure to apply enough paint to kill the bright bronze color of Kadee (and other) metal coupler springs. Follow this with lighter rust colors applied by dry-brushing or artist's crayons.

The prototype photo highlights other details as well, including the dull gray air hose and lighter metal piping and parts. Some of the weathering will get scratched off in service, but that will look realistic on couplers.

Painting structures

Improving the realism of any kit

Painting structures isn't much different from painting freight cars or loco-motives. One difference is that you usually have a lot more leeway in choosing colors and designs of structures, because you're free to free-lance (unless you're modeling a specific real building).

The important thing is to keep the colors realistic. Remember that, with few exceptions, structures are painted in flat tones. Since most model structures are molded in plastic, you'll have to paint your structures to get a truly realistic look—even if the box or package boasts that the kit is "molded in realistic colors." Painting your structures will make them more realistic, and by varying the color schemes and details you can have a building that's different from all the other similar kits out there.

SIMULATING BRICK

Brick is a common building material in real life, especially in the older parts of towns and cities (where railroads tend to run). Many injection-molded structures and kits are molded with brick texture, including storefront buildings and industrial structures.

Paint structures in subassemblies if possible. To avoid having glue ooze out of a joint and ruin the paint job, assemble the structure as much as possible before painting. If a structure has separate window castings, roof, and other details, leave them off and paint them separately.

Start by painting the walls a base brick color. Real bricks come in many colors, including several shades of red and brown, as well as cream and beige. In addition, some brick buildings have been painted—many in non-traditional colors for brick.

Fig. 9-1. Start by painting the walls a basic brick color. Boxcar red, oxide red, and mineral red are all good choices.

Fig. 9-2. Prototype brick and mortar colors vary from building to building.

Fig. 9-3. Give the brick a wash of the mortar color.

Fig. 9-4. The finished wash effect is good, but the wash sometimes creeps onto the brick faces.

You can use a brush, as in fig. 9-1, but an airbrush or spray can will also give good results. I picked a shade of boxcar red.

Mortar color can vary almost as much as the bricks themselves, as the real building in fig. 9-2 shows. Rarely is mortar bright white—instead it is usually a shade of gray, sometimes reddish-gray.

The most common way to simulate mortar is to give the bricks a wash of the mortar color, as fig. 9-3 shows. Start with a mix of about one part paint to six or seven parts thin-

ner (in general, the darker the color, the more thinner to use).

Figure 9-4 shows the results. Note how the effect is quite good when you look at the structure as a whole. Upon close inspection, however, you can see that the wash tends to creep up on many brick faces.

You can fix this, as fig. 9-5 shows, by lightly rubbing the brick surface with a pencil eraser. This will remove the wash color from the brick faces, but leave the wash color in the mortar lines.

You can stop here and have a

pretty good brick structure, but you can also take the detailing to another level. Since individual bricks often vary in color, as the prototype photos show, adding these different colors to a model greatly enhances its appearance.

Figure 9-6 shows how. Use a fine-point brush to paint bricks randomly with different colors. Two or three additional colors are all it takes to create a nice effect. Figure 9-7 shows the final results on one building.

Fig. 9-5. Rubbing lightly with a pencil eraser will remove traces of the wash from the brick faces.

Fig. 9-6. On some structures paint random bricks with different shades of red.

Fig. 9-7. Here's a finished structure with random brick colors.

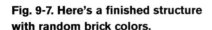

PAINTING DETAILS

Many structures, such as DPM's storefront buildings, have windows, cornices, iron fronts, and other details molded in place. Paint the bricks as on other structures, then use a brush to paint the details, as fig. 9-8 shows.

Figure 9-9 shows the results of doing this on two structures. Painting windows and other details takes some time, but the appearance of a building with varied and realistic colors is quite impressive.

Fig. 9-8. Use a fine brush to paint plastic structures' cast-on details.

Fig. 9-9. Varying brick and trim colors help give each building a unique appearance.

WOOD STRUCTURES

There are many excellent wood kits on the market, ranging from craftsman-style structures to laser-cut kits that go together almost as easily as a plastic kit.

Examine all the wood parts before painting, and remove any fuzz, burrs, or imperfections with fine sandpaper or a hobby knife. Paint as many items as possible before you assemble the kit.

I like to give all wood parts a coat of latex primer (fig. 9-10) or sanding sealer. This cuts down on the chance that wood grain or other imperfections will show through and makes it easier to get an even coat of the final color.

Once the primer is dry, paint the finish color with either an airbrush or brush. It's best to apply a couple of light coats. Don't apply the paint too heavily, or the wood pieces will tend to warp or bow. If this happens, add plenty of interior bracing during assembly. Figure 9-11 shows a finished American Model Builders wood depot.

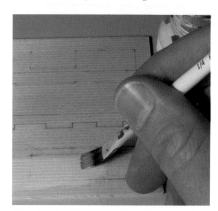

Fig. 9-10. Give wood parts a coat of primer before painting the final color. This is common latex primer.

Fig. 9-11. This American Model Builders wood depot was painted Polly Scale Mineral Red.

Signs

Signs are an important element for structures, giving them a lot of visual interest. They are also a key way to give your buildings a unique look. There are a few ways to add signs to structures.

One method is with decals. Microscale and others make a wide variety of sign decals for storefront and industrial buildings as well as gas stations and restaurants.

However, one of my favorite methods of creating the look of a painted-on sign (such as on the D.P. Wigley building) is to use dry transfers as a mask. The photos show how I did this with a Berghoff Beer sign on a plastic storefront building.

Start by painting the lettering color (usually white) on a panel of the structure as large as the final sign will be. Let the paint dry.

Rub the dry transfers in place, using just enough pressure to get the lettering to stick. The Berghoff lettering is from a Clover House billboard refrigerator car set; alphabet sets work just as well.

Airbrush the background color (black, in this case) over the panel in very light coats. The dry transfers will act like a mask, keeping the background color off the underlying white paint.

Once the paint is dry, press masking tape firmly in place over the dry transfers. When the tape is peeled away, the dry transfers will come with it, leaving a painted sign behind. You might have to do a bit of touchup with a knife and small brush if some paint has crept under a transfer or if small pieces of the transfer stick to the structure.

This technique was also used on the Joyce Lumber Co. building in fig. 9-7.

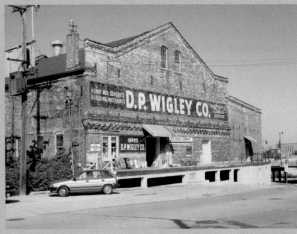

Making plastic look like wood

Many plastic kits are molded to represent unpainted wood. This deck from an Accurail bridge kit is one example. Start by giving the surface a uniform flat coat of paint—I used grimy black for the bridge deck.

Making the surface look like wood is a matter of adding and blending other colors—usually browns, tans, and black, depending on whether the effect is to represent treated or untreated wood, and how old the wood is supposed to be.

You can use paint washes or drybrushing to do this, but for this bridge deck I used brown, black, and light tan chalk to highlight individual boards and areas of boards.

I followed this with streaks of black where the wheels of vehicles would have worn and weathered the surface. Follow the chalk weathering with a coat of clear flat. You can see the difference between the unpainted plastic deck and the weathered one in the photo at lower right.

Painting figures and vehicles

Adding life to your layout

When modelers think about painting, it's usually the big items that get attention: locomotives, rolling stock, and structures. However, how we treat detail items goes a long way toward increasing the realism of a layout or scene.

There are a tremendous number of detail items on the market, particularly in HO scale. The selection of details in N and other scales is growing rapidly. Here's a look at how to paint and detail some of them.

TEN

FIGURES

Several companies make nicely detailed plastic figures. Preiser, probably the best-known company, makes a wide variety in scales from Z to G. Cast-metal figures are also available from a variety of manufacturers.

One of the main reasons to paint your own figures is price: A box of six painted Preiser figures costs around $8, but you can buy a set of 120 undecorated Preiser figures for about $20. With a bit of patience and a steady hand, you can populate a layout inexpensively—and have much better-looking figures to boot. You can also use these techniques to repaint any pre-painted commercial figure.

One problem with most factory-painted figures is the finish. All too often figures have a high-gloss sheen, and in colors that range from grotesque to unpleasant. Painting your own figures ensures that your miniature people will have the look you want.

The HO scale Preiser people in fig. 10-1 come several to a sprue, which makes a handy handle for working and painting. Begin by cleaning any flash or mold lines with a knife, as fig. 10-2 shows. When that's done, scrub the figures with warm water and dish detergent (to get rid of any oils from handling) and let them dry.

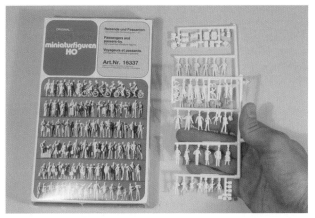

Fig. 10-1. Preiser offers several sets of unpainted figures, and other companies also offer unpainted people.

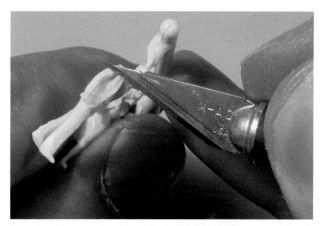

Fig. 10-2. Use a knife to clean any mold lines and flash from the castings.

PAINTING

The basic technique of painting is to spray the figures with a skin color, then use fine-point brushes to paint clothes, shoes, and hair.

Airbrush the entire sprue of figures with a flesh color. For caucasian skin I usually start with a Polly Scale mix of two parts 505212 Flesh and one part Reefer White. Thin this mix with 25 percent Polly S Airbrush Thinner for spraying.

You can give individual figures (or groups of figures) suntans and varying skin tones by giving them light oversprays of grimy black paint or by mixing Grimy Black with the flesh mix before airbrushing. For African-American skin, mix Polly Scale Roof Brown, Flesh, Grimy Black, and Black to achieve various shades. Other good flesh tones are Modelflex 16204 Light Flesh, 16205 Medium Flesh, and 16206 Dark Flesh.

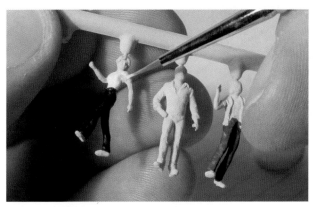

Fig. 10-3. Paint clothing and other details while the figures are still attached to the sprues.

Fig. 10-4. Craft paints work well for painting figures.

Now comes the fun part. Using fine-point brushes, paint individual details, as fig. 10-3 shows. Use water-based flat colors. My favorite paints for figures are craft paints, as shown in fig. 10-4. They have a smooth consistency, are easy to work with, brush well, and dry flat. Polly Scale and Pactra Acrylic Enamel flat paints also work well.

Keep your brush wet with paint, and push the paint carefully to the raised lines that define edges of clothing. If you go over an edge, don't worry—simply touch it up later.

Be sure to keep clothing colors consistent with the era you're modeling. Solid-color clothes are the easiest to paint. Stripes and patterns are difficult, but if you have a steady hand, they can be done.

When you've finished with the clothing and the paint is dry, use a sprue cutter to separate the figure from the sprue, then clean up that area with a hobby knife.

Paint the hair. I put several colors on a piece of scrap plastic, mixing them to get a wide variety of colors. For blond hair, use a mix of yellow, white, and brown, and vary the mix among figures. See fig. 10-5. For darker hair color you can use any color from black to light brown.

I've found the best way to highlight lips and eyebrows is with a pencil, as shown in fig. 10-6. It's impossible to control paint in such a small area, and these details should be subtle. Trying to paint these with a brush, even in O scale, usually results in a clown face. A standard graphite or brown pencil works well for most figures, but you can use a red pencil for creating lipstick on a dressed-up female figure.

Figure 10-7 shows several completed figures. These techniques are applicable to figures in any scale, even small N scale ones as shown. Since painting figures takes a bit of time, save your best efforts for foreground scenes where they're readily visible. Great detail isn't needed for figures in background scenes or large groups.

Fig. 10-5. Paint hair with a mix of yellow, white, brown, and black paints.

Fig. 10-6. Use a pencil (plain graphite or red) for highlighting lips, eyes, and eyebrows.

Fig. 10-7. These techniques work well on figures of all scales, as shown by these HO and N scale people.

VEHICLES

The number of high-quality ready-to-run vehicles has grown rapidly in the past few years, and many kits are still available. We'll go through painting and highlighting a few kits, but you can use the same techniques to repaint or touch up ready-to-run vehicles as well.

Model vehicle kits are generally made of three materials: injection-molded styrene, cast urethane or polyester resin, or cast metal. Figure 10-8 shows four HO scale vehicles: a Magnuson Models (Walthers) resin grain truck and car, an Alloy Forms metal pickup truck, and a Williams Bros. styrene car.

Regardless of the material, the steps for treating vehicles are about the same. The first step is taking care of any surface irregularities. On injection-molded styrene cars, this usually means cleaning flash or touching up mold parting lines. On cast-metal and resin vehicles, this can include filling and sanding any imperfections or pock marks in the body, as fig. 10-9 shows.

As with other models, scrub the vehicles thoroughly in dish detergent and warm water. This is especially important with resin vehicles. Allow them to air-dry.

Cars and trucks in real life generally have waxed, glossy surfaces, so models usually look more realistic if they have at least a semi-gloss sheen. The exceptions to this include old clunkers with oxidized surfaces and dirty or grimy vehicles.

I airbrushed the wheels/tires for all the vehicles at once, then painted the wheels and hubcaps various colors, as shown in fig. 10-10.

Here's how I painted each of the four vehicles, with some hints on working with the various materials.

Grain truck. I airbrushed the truck with Polly Scale Caboose Red. In airbrushing acrylic paint on resin, it's important to apply the paint in very thin coats—but make

Fig. 10-8. A wide variety of vehicle kits are available, including this HO (clockwise from upper left) resin Magnuson (Walthers) grain truck and car, clear styrene Williams Bros. car, and cast metal Alloy Forms pickup truck.

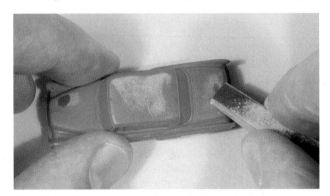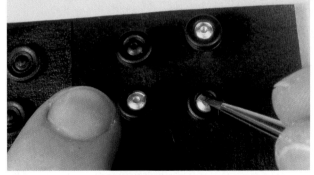

Fig. 10-9. Fix any surface imperfections before painting the castings.

Fig. 10-10. Paint wheels and other detail items separately.

sure the paint is wet when it hits the surface. If you apply the paint too heavily, it will bead up on the surface. If this happens, quickly wash it off under hot water while scrubbing it with a toothbrush. Allow the model to dry, then try again. I used a hair dryer on the paint to speed the drying time between each coat.

Figure 10-11 shows how to do the grillwork on the front. Start by painting the grill area (including the depressed background areas) black, then use the side of a brush to paint the grill itself the proper color (white, in this case). This is a great technique for creating a look of depth in grills.

Brush-paint the wheel centers UP Harbor Mist Gray and the tarp on the truck box Grimy Black.

Windows on cast-resin vehicles are a challenge, since the vehicles are usually cast in an opaque color. On this model I started by painting the window areas silver, then adding washes of blue, followed by a couple of coats of clear gloss.

I've also had excellent results painting windows Testor's Sapphire, a metallic dark blue color. The paint dries glossy, and the final effect is that of reflected sky. Figure 10-12 shows an example.

Finish with details: Polly S Flat Aluminum on the cab-roof lamp housings, door handles, and headlights; and orange on the cab-roof lamps.

Chevy Bel Air. Treat this resin car like the grain truck. I started by airbrushing the roof Polly Scale Antique White. When this dried, I masked off the roof area and sprayed the rest of the car L&N Blue.

Use a fine-point brush and Testor's Silver to paint the grill. Use the edge of a brush to carefully outline the strips on the side and the "Bel Air" lettering on the rear sides. Treat the windows like those of the grain truck.

I painted the sidewalls white, keeping the brush wet and allowing the paint to flow to the separation mark on the tire. If a bit creeps over the line, touch it up later with a little black.

Ford pickup. Use small files and a hobby knife to clean up the

Fig. 10-11. Paint the grill black, then use the side of a brush to paint the grill color on the raised areas. Some touchup will probably be required.

Fig. 10-12. Testor's Sapphire enamel works well for painting windows on solid castings.

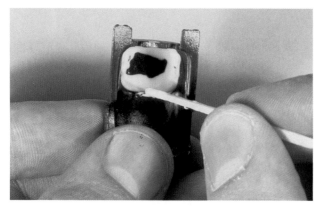

Fig. 10-13. To use Micro Krystal Klear for windows, paint it around the edge of the window, then use a toothpick to pull the film across the window opening.

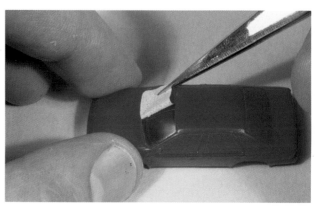

Fig. 10-14. For clear styrene or resin vehicles, mask the windows before painting. Removing the mask reveals the clear windows.

window openings and any other areas on the body.

Airbrush the cab and box separately with Polly Scale Engine Black before assembly. Use a fine-point brush to paint the grille white and the door handles and name plates (on the sides of the hood) flat aluminum.

Many plastic vehicles include clear plastic molded to fit window openings, but you're on your own for metal vehicles. Microscale Micro Krystal Klear comes in handy for window glazing, and fig. 10-13 shows how I did it on the pickup. The technique comes in handy in other applications as well.

Assemble the pickup using cyanoacrylate adhesive (CA).

Ford Taurus. One advantage of clear styrene vehicles like those from Williams is that windows are easy. Place masking tape over the windows and press it firmly in place. Use a hobby knife to cut along the window lines, then remove the excess tape.

Airbrush the car the desired color (Modelflex Signal Red on this one). Once the paint's dry, peel off the window masking, as in fig. 10-14.

Use a brush to highlight details, as you did on the other vehicles. To make the black strip along the side, I used a scrap piece of black decal stripe.

Other options. You can also use vehicle touch-up paint (fig.

10-15) to paint urethane and metal vehicles. This lacquer-based paint is designed for touching up paint on real cars and trucks; it is available in a variety of colors that match—of course—real vehicle colors. They can be found at auto parts stores as well as many car dealerships.

Brush the paint onto the model, making sure the surface is covered around all details. Don't try to cover the model in one coat—it might take two or three coats for complete coverage. Be sure to use adequate ventilation when using these paints.

Detailing trucks and trailers. There are a number of details you can add to commercial vehicles,

 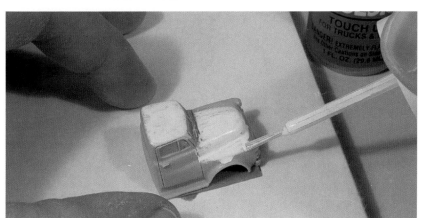

Fig. 10-15. Vehicle touch-up paint can be used to paint resin and cast-metal vehicle models.

especially trucks and truck trailers. Figure 10-16 shows a stock factory-painted trailer next to one that's been detailed.

Good decal sets for improving vehicles are Microscale set nos. 87-852 (HO scale) and 60-852 (N scale), which include marker lights, trailer builder's plates, mud flap lettering, placards, and other typical trailer markings; and MC-4168 and MC-4149 (HO), which are vehicle license plates.

You can also paint the wheels. The original wheels on the upgraded trailer in fig. 10-16 were replaced by new ones from Athearn.

If the vehicle has raised lettering, like the old Lindberg truck in fig. 10-17, you can paint the body a contrasting color from the mold-ing, then scrape the paint away from the lettering to highlight the lettering.

The finished truck also shows how marker lights and door handles can be highlighted with paint. The grill has also been painted black in the recessed areas, and a seated figure has been added to the cab.

Fig. 10-16. A few decals and some paint makes the trailer at right much more realistic than the stock factory-painted Walthers trailer at left.

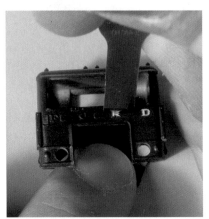

Fig. 10-17. Highlight raised lettering by painting the body a contrasting color, then scraping the paint from the letters. Other highlights include painted marker lights, grill, and door latch.

Suppliers and manufacturers

DECALS AND DRY TRANSFERS

Accu-cals, SMP Industries, 63 Hudson Rd., P. O. Box 72, Bolton, MA 01740: HO scale decals for northeastern U.S. and Canadian railroads

Blair Line, P. O. Box 1136, Carthage, MO 64836-1136, www.blairline.com: graffiti decals

CDS Lettering Ltd., P. O. Box 78003 Cityview, Nepean, Ontario K2G 5W2: N, HO, S, and O scale dry transfers for North American railroads, with an emphasis on Canada

Champion Decal Co., P. O. Box 1178, Minot, ND 58702, www.minndaklite.com: HO and O scale decals for North American railroads, specializing in steam and early diesel eras

Clover House, P. O. Box 62, Sebastopol, CA 95473-0062: N, HO, S, and O scale dry transfers for turn-of-the-century through late-steam-era railroads

Greg Komar Dry Transfers, 15532 Woodway Dr., Tampa, FL 33613-1132: dry transfers for U.S. railroads

Microscale Industries, 18435 Bandilier Circle, Fountain Valley, CA 92708, www.microscale.com: N, HO, S, O, and G scale decals for North American railroads

Oddballs Custom Decals, 26550 227th St., McLouth, KS 66054, www.oddballsdecals.com: N and HO scale diesel-era decals for U.S. railroads

ShellScale Decals, 516 Houston Mines Rd., Troutville, VA 24175: HO scale number board decals and N, HO, and O scale decals for Norfolk Southern and predecessors

Wm. K. Walthers, P. O. Box 18676, Milwaukee, WI 53218, www.walthers.com: N, HO, and O scale decals for North American railroads

AIRBRUSH EQUIPMENT

Badger Air-Brush Co., 9128 W. Belmont Ave., Franklin Park, IL 60131, www.badger-airbrush.com: airbrushes, compressors, spray booths, and related equipment

North Coast Models, P. O. Box 31, McKees Rocks, PA 15136: spray booths and air-abrasive blasters

Paasche Airbrush Co., 7440 W. Lawrence Ave., Harwood Heights, IL 60656, www.thomasregister.com/paasche: airbrushes, compressors, spray booths, and related equipment

W. R. Brown Co., 901 E. 22nd St., North Chicago, IL 60064: airbrushes, compressors, spray booths, and related equipment

PAINT

Accu-paint, SMP Industries, 63 Hudson Rd., P. O. Box 72, Bolton, MA 01740

Floquil, see Testor

Modelflex (Badger), 9128 W. Belmont Ave., Franklin Park, IL 60131, www.badger-airbrush.com

Pactra, 1000 Lake Road, Medina, OH 44256

Polly Scale, Polly S, see Testor

Scalecoat, Quality Craft Models, 177 Wheatley Ave., Northumberland, PA 17857

Testor Corp., 620 Buckbee St., Rockford, IL 61104, www.testors.com

OTHER MANUFACTURERS

Loew-Cornell Inc., 563 Chestnut Ave., Teaneck, NJ 07666-2490, www.loew-cornell.com: brushes, artist's chalks, and art supplies

Index